Vintage Ladies

Coloring Book

by Christea Blue

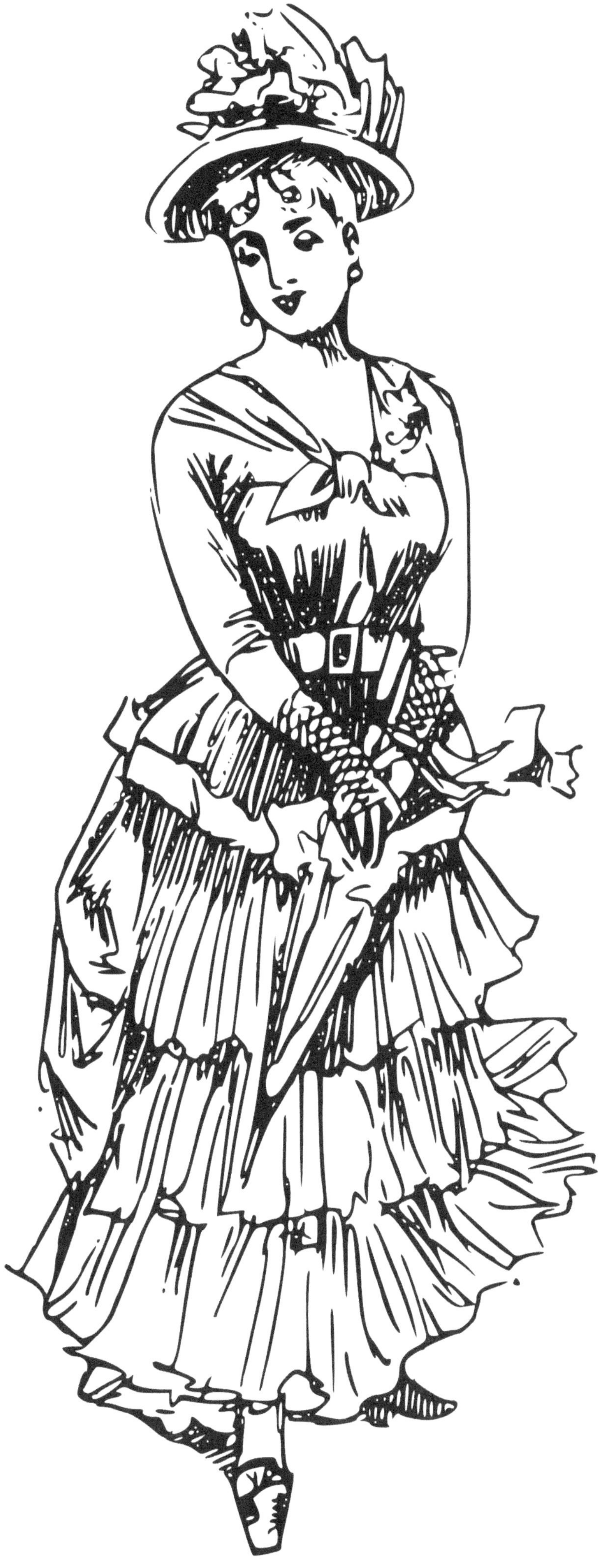

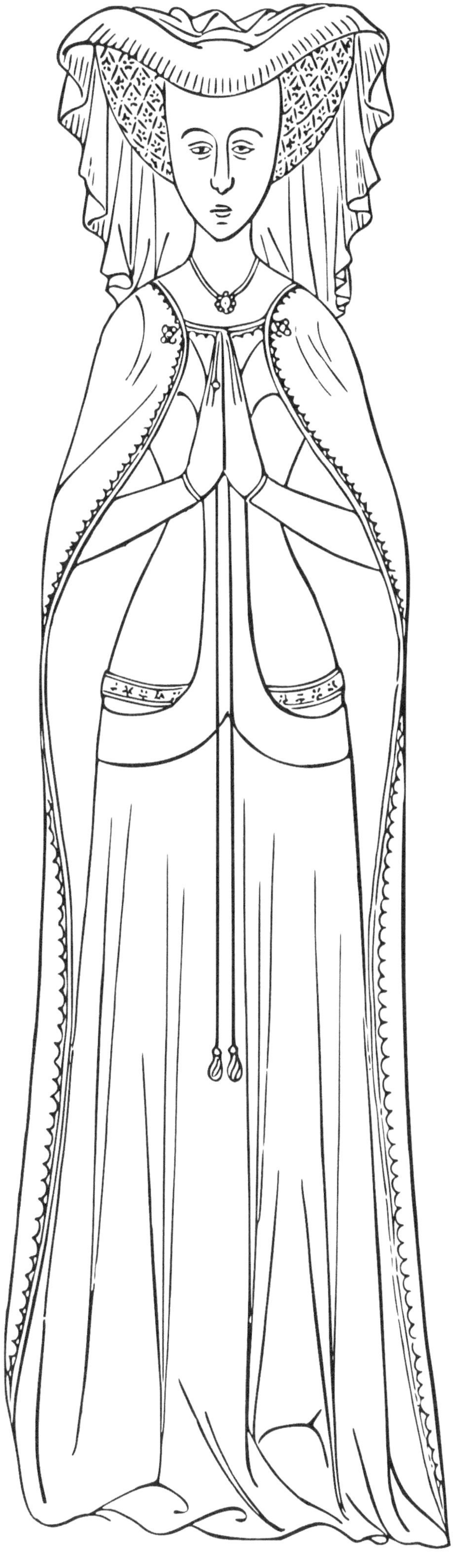

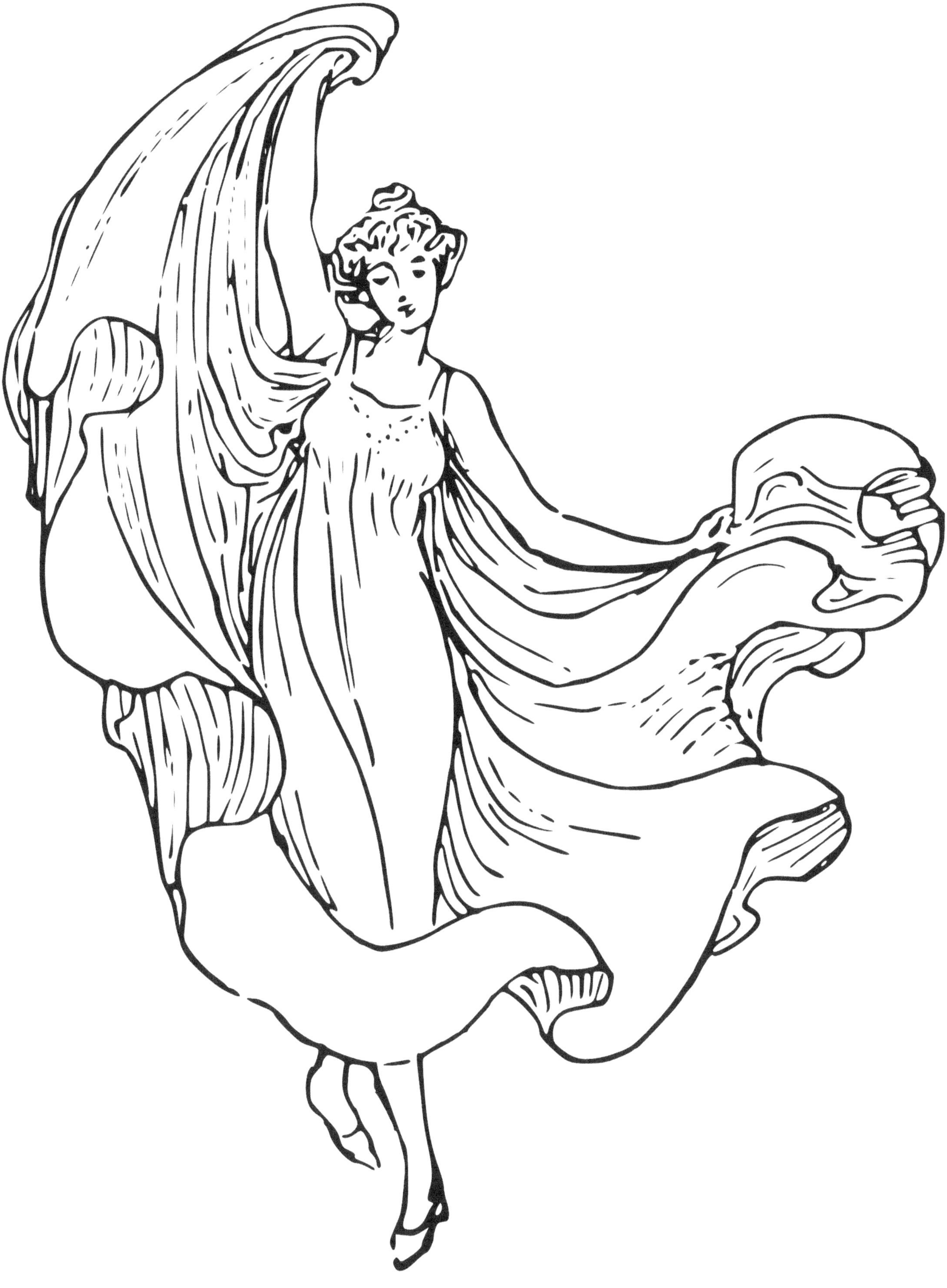

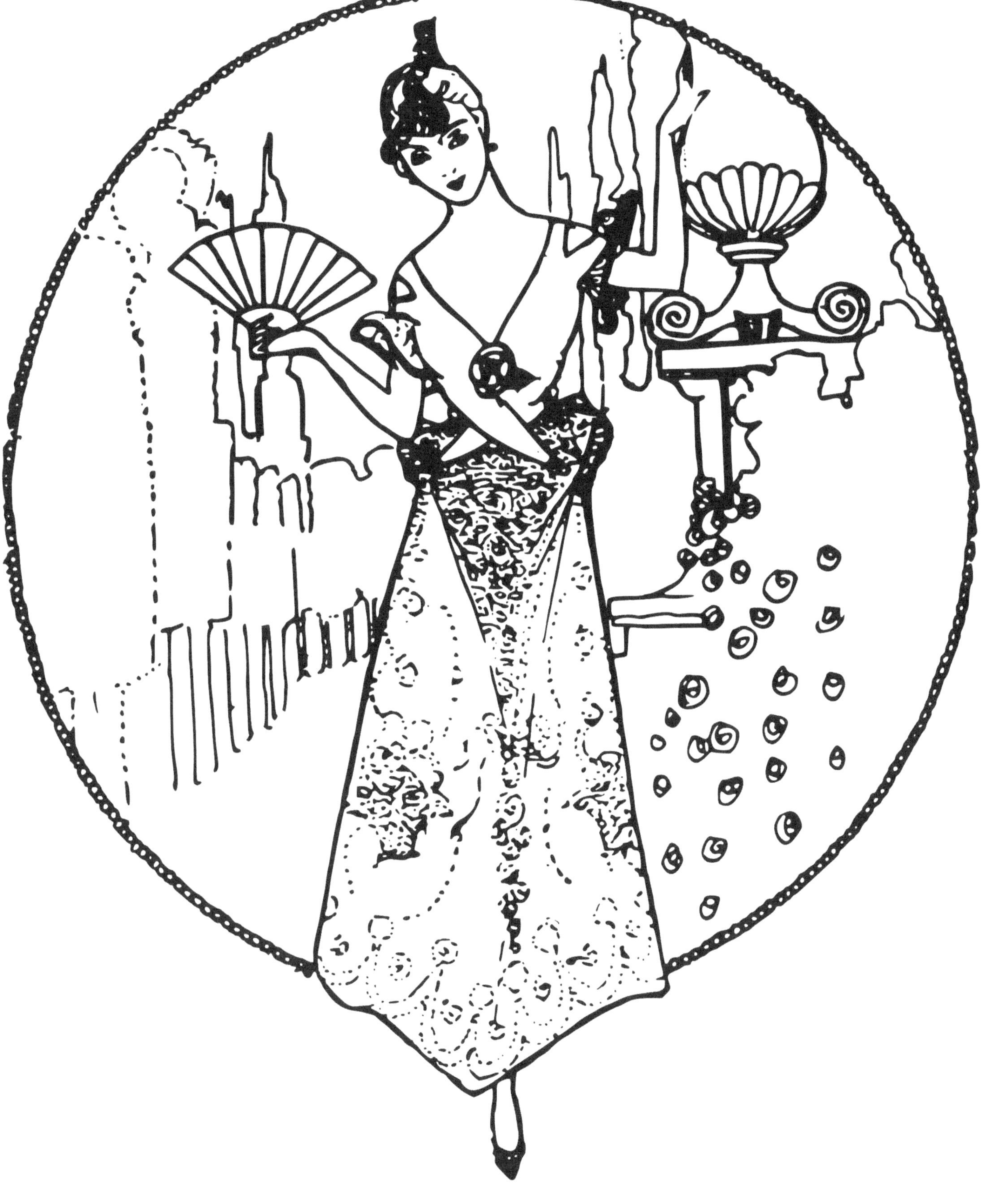

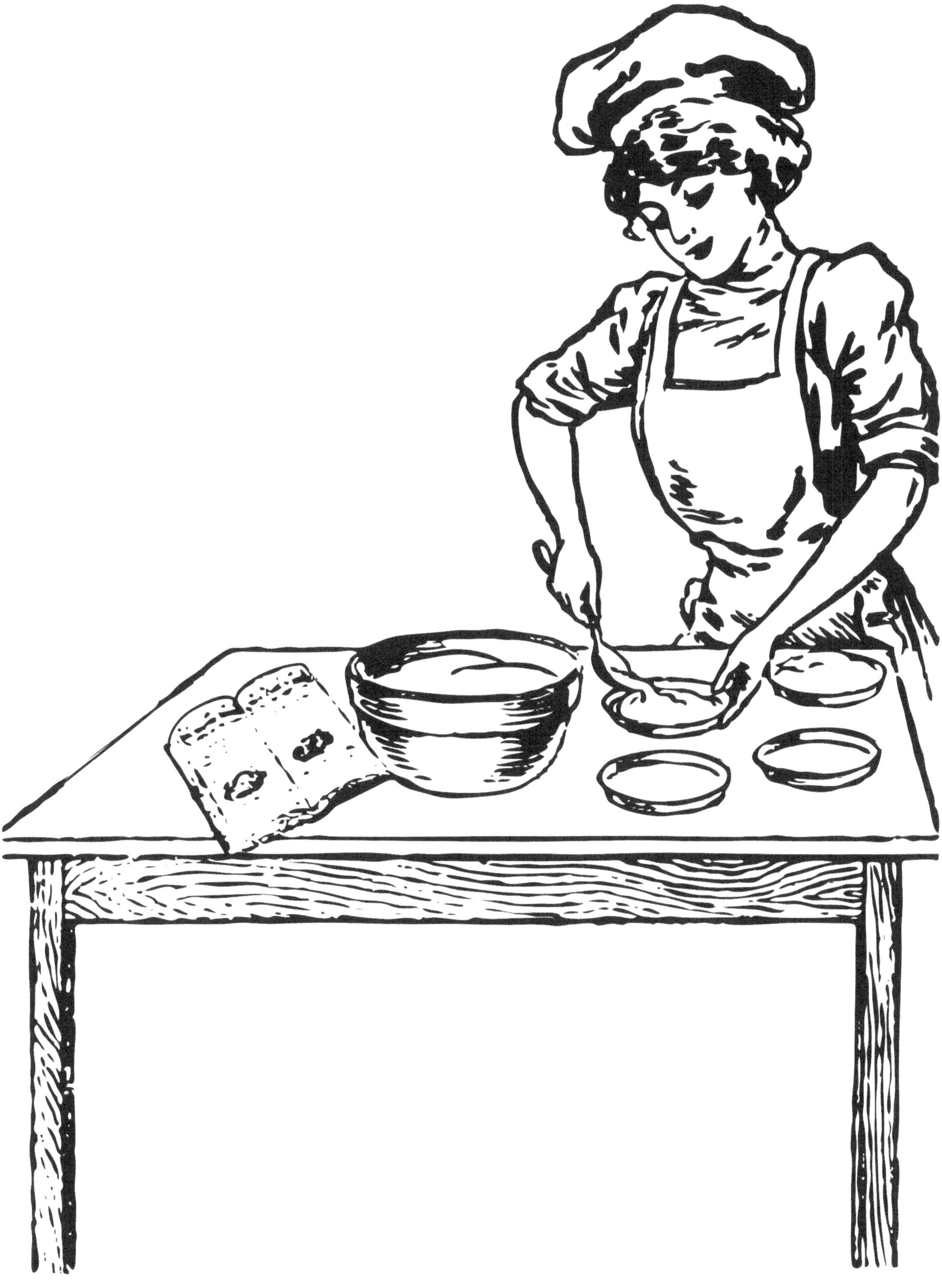

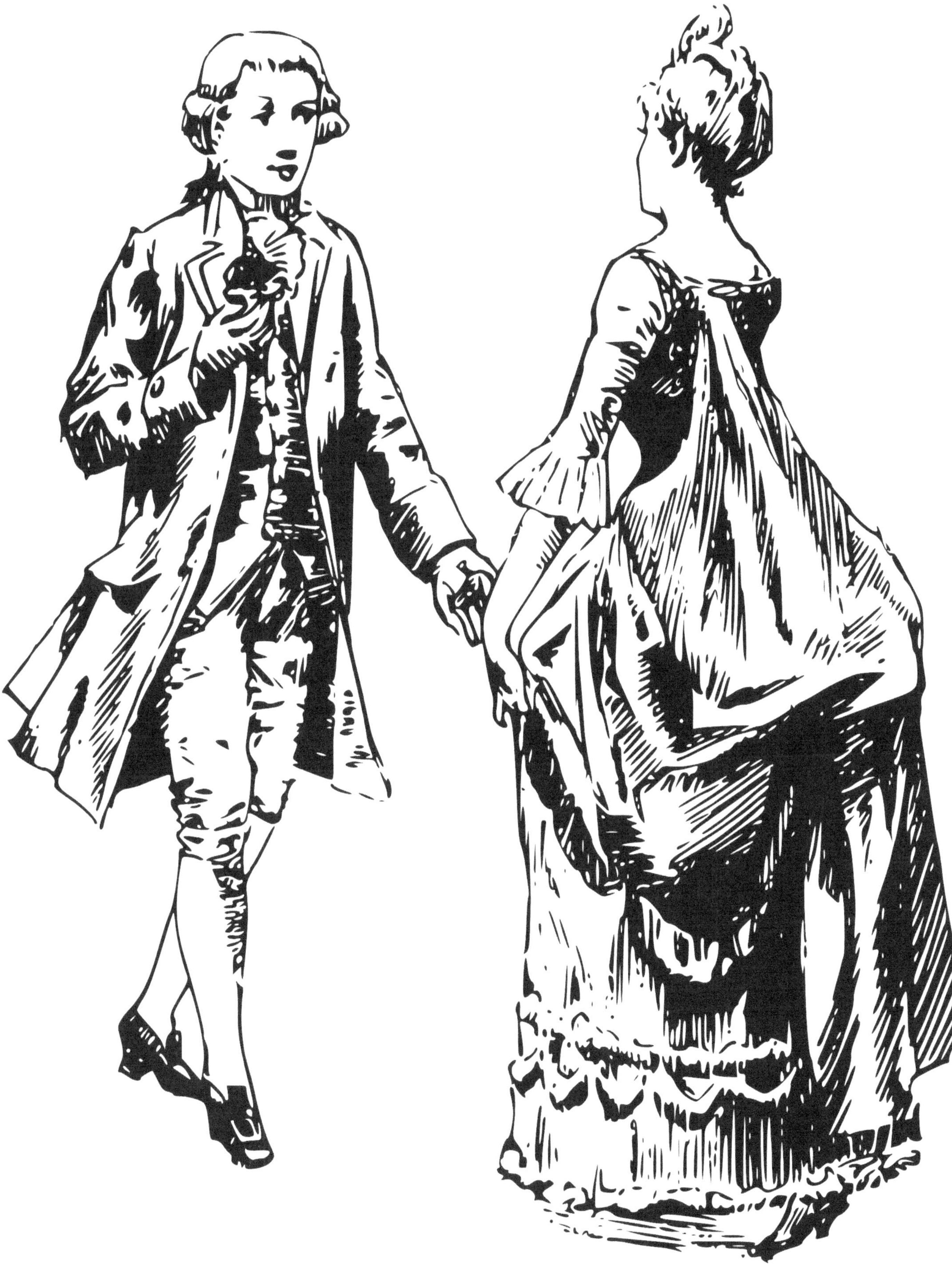

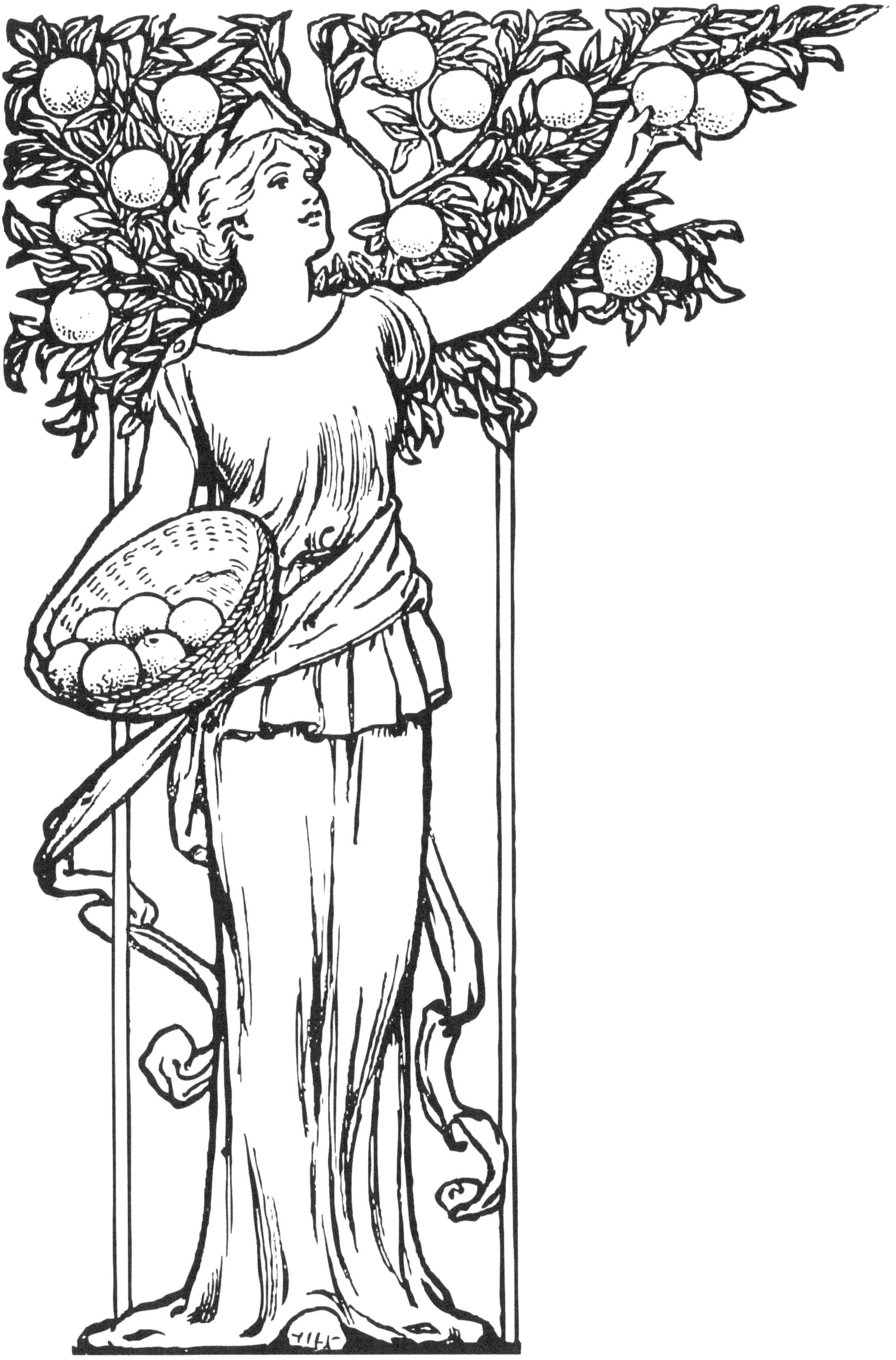

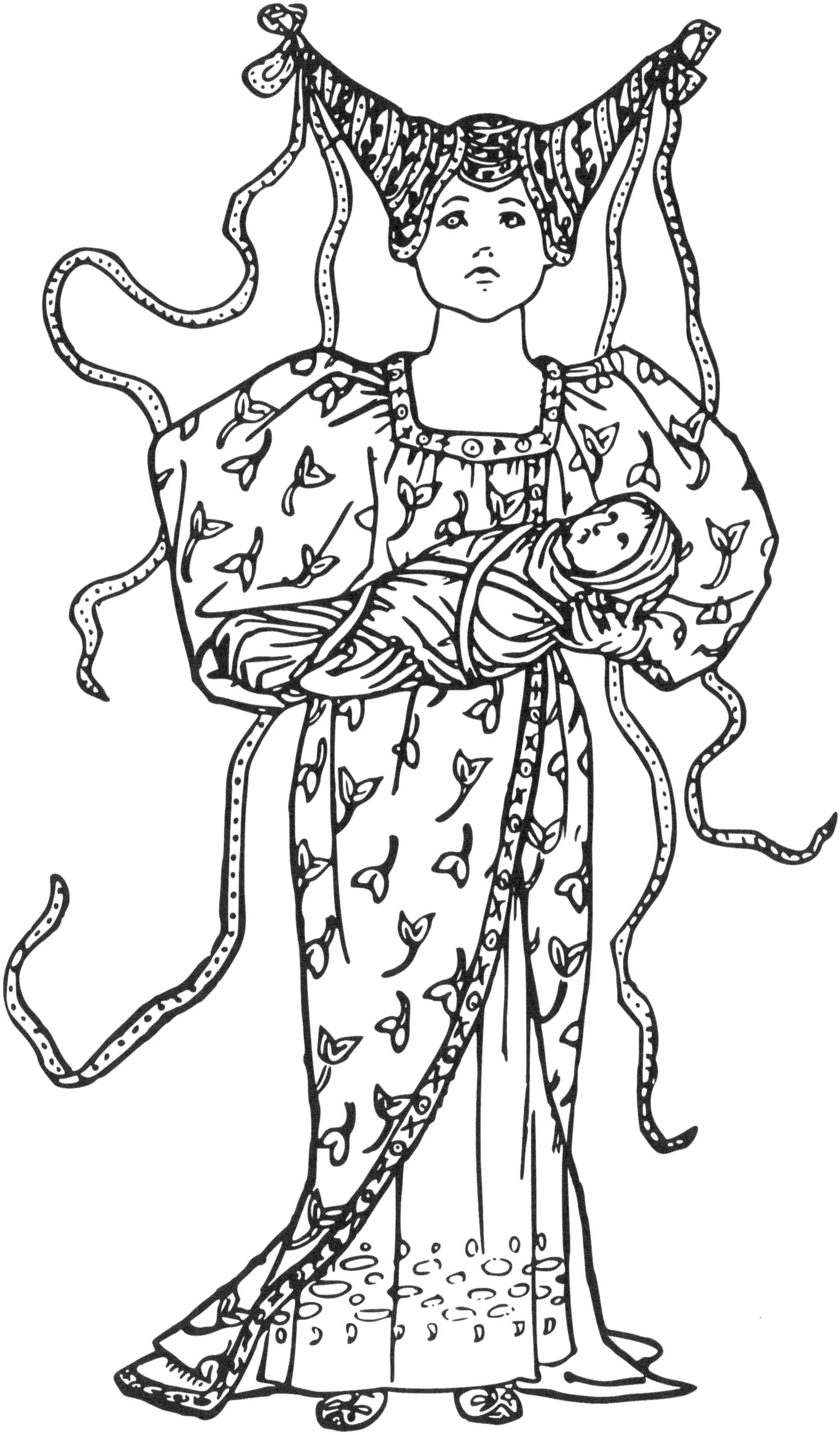

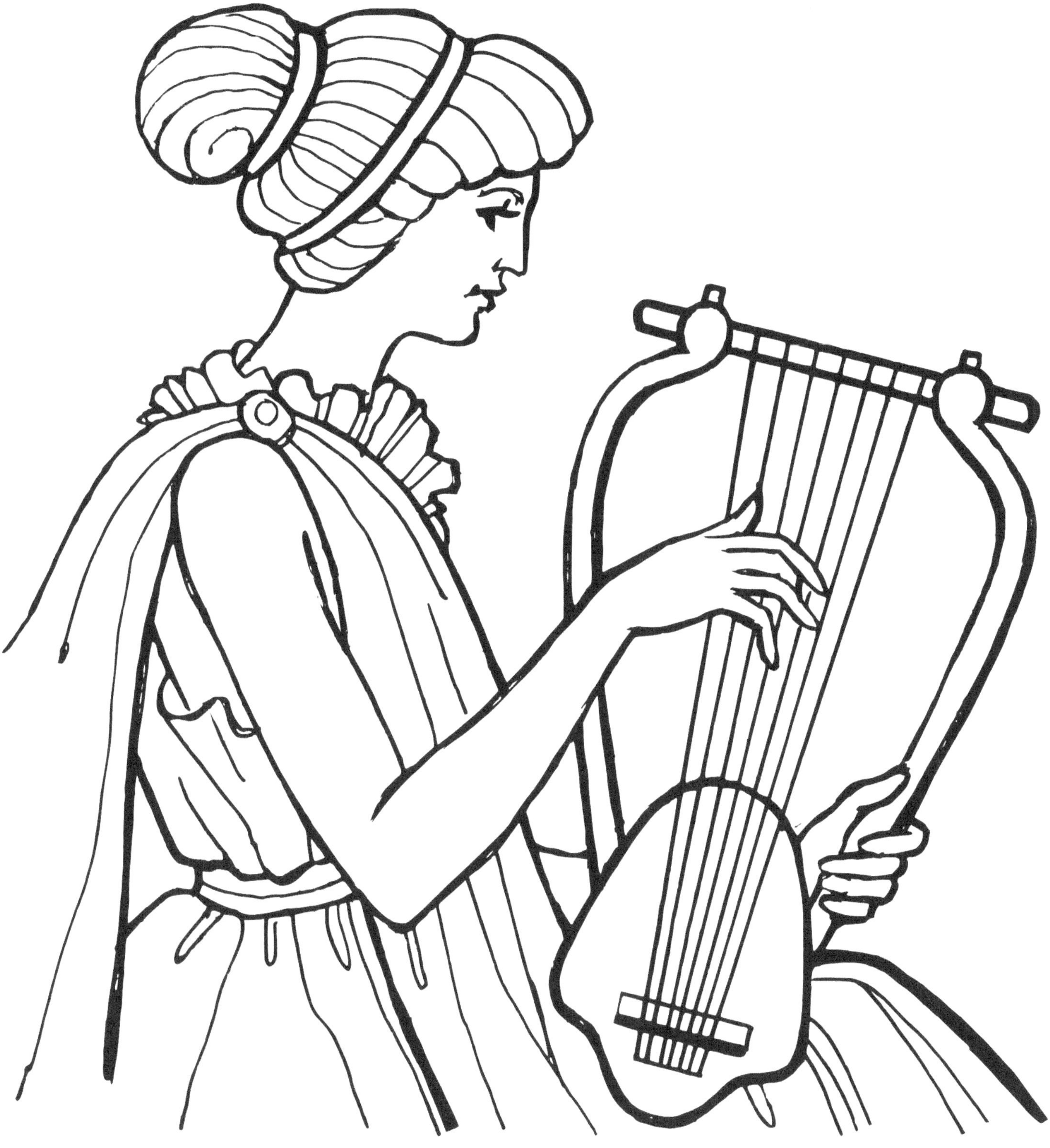

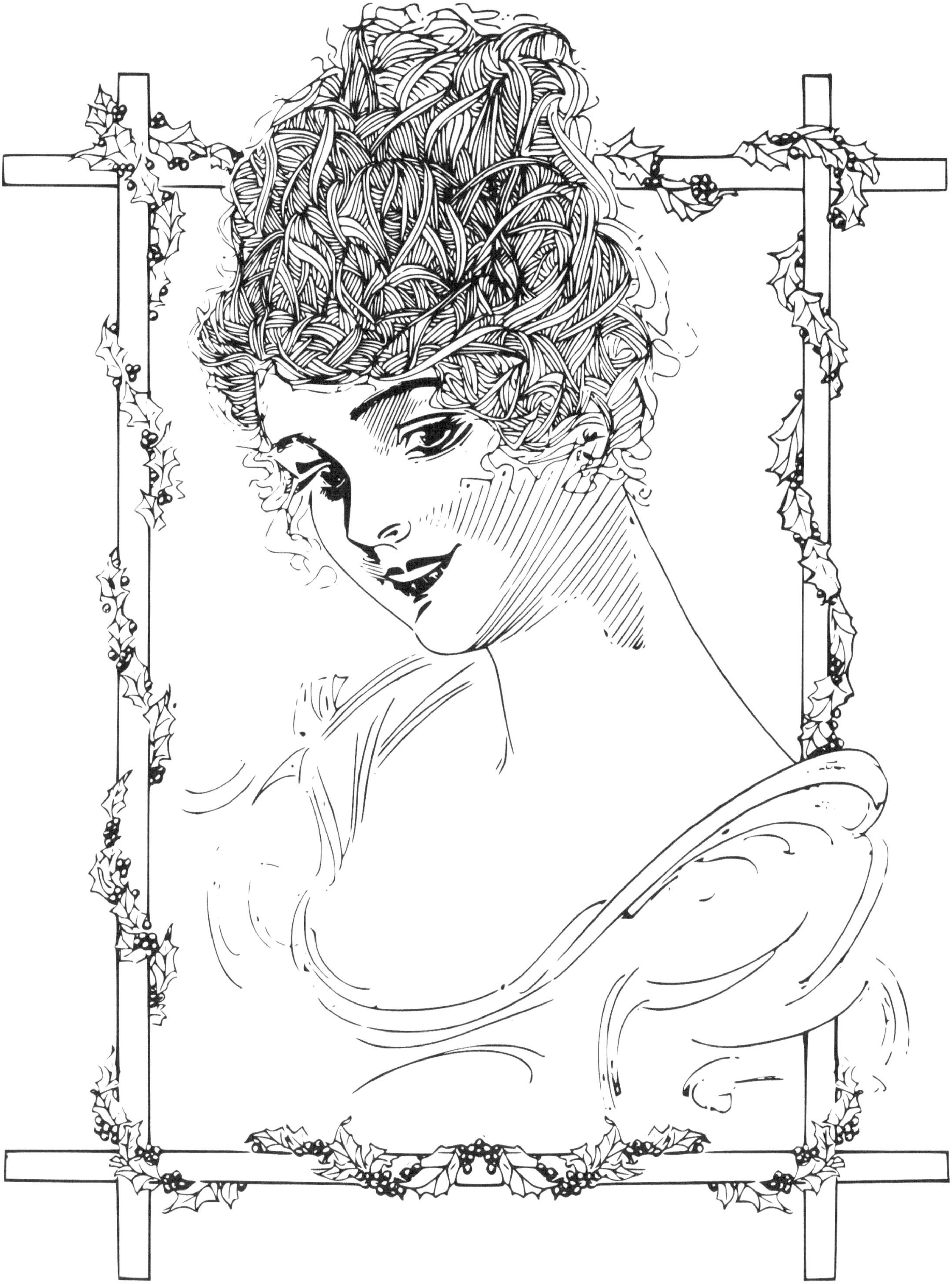

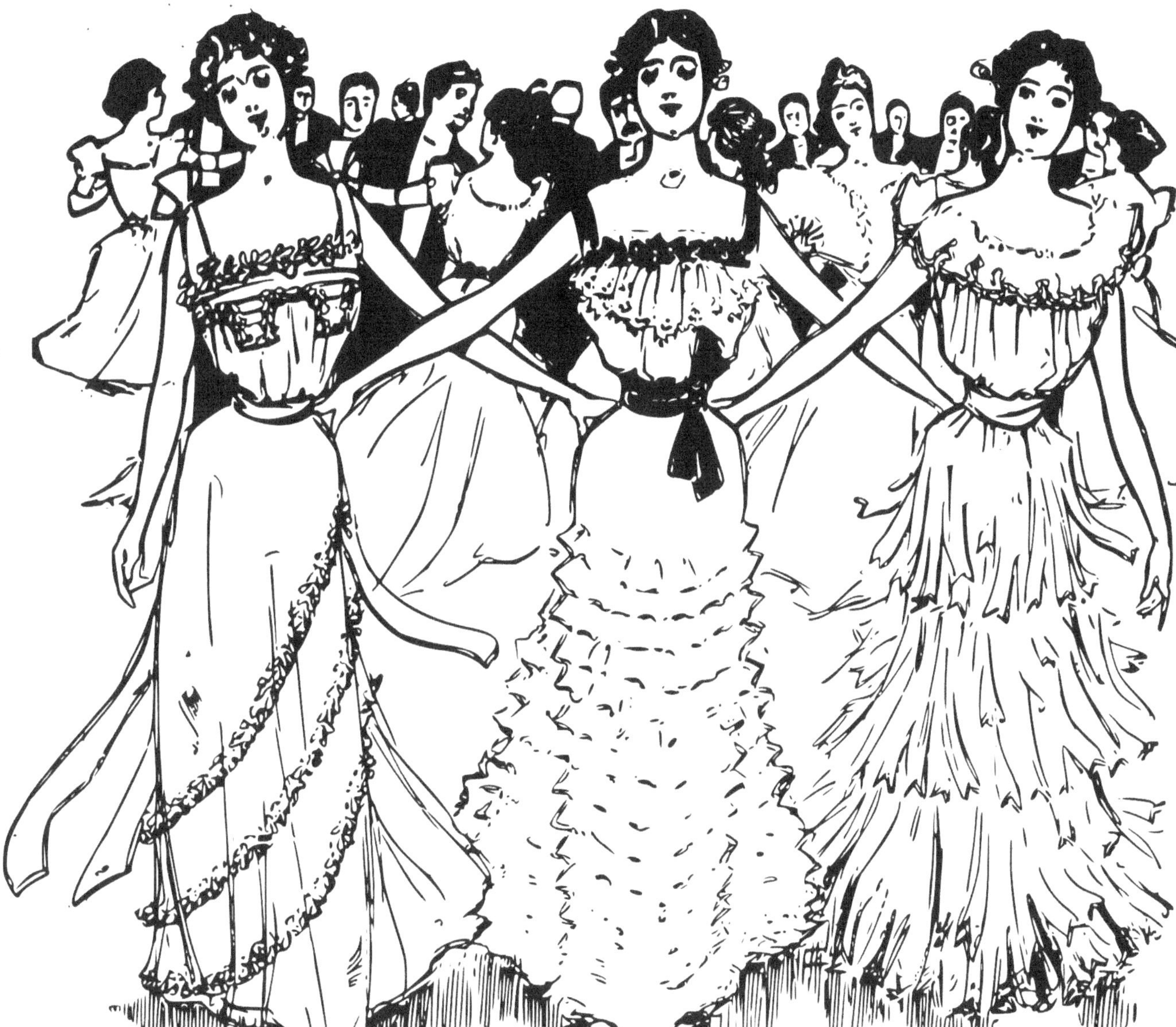

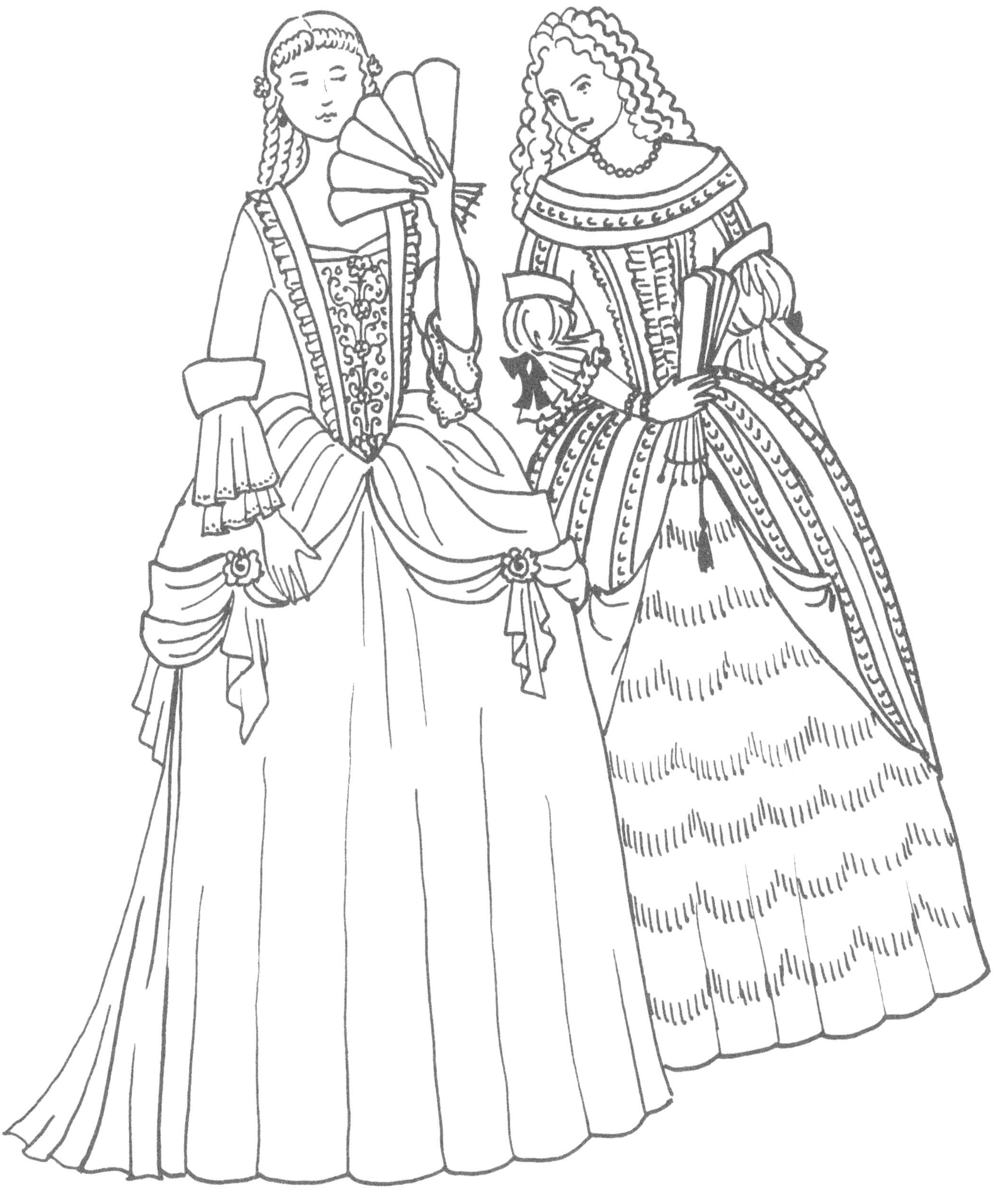

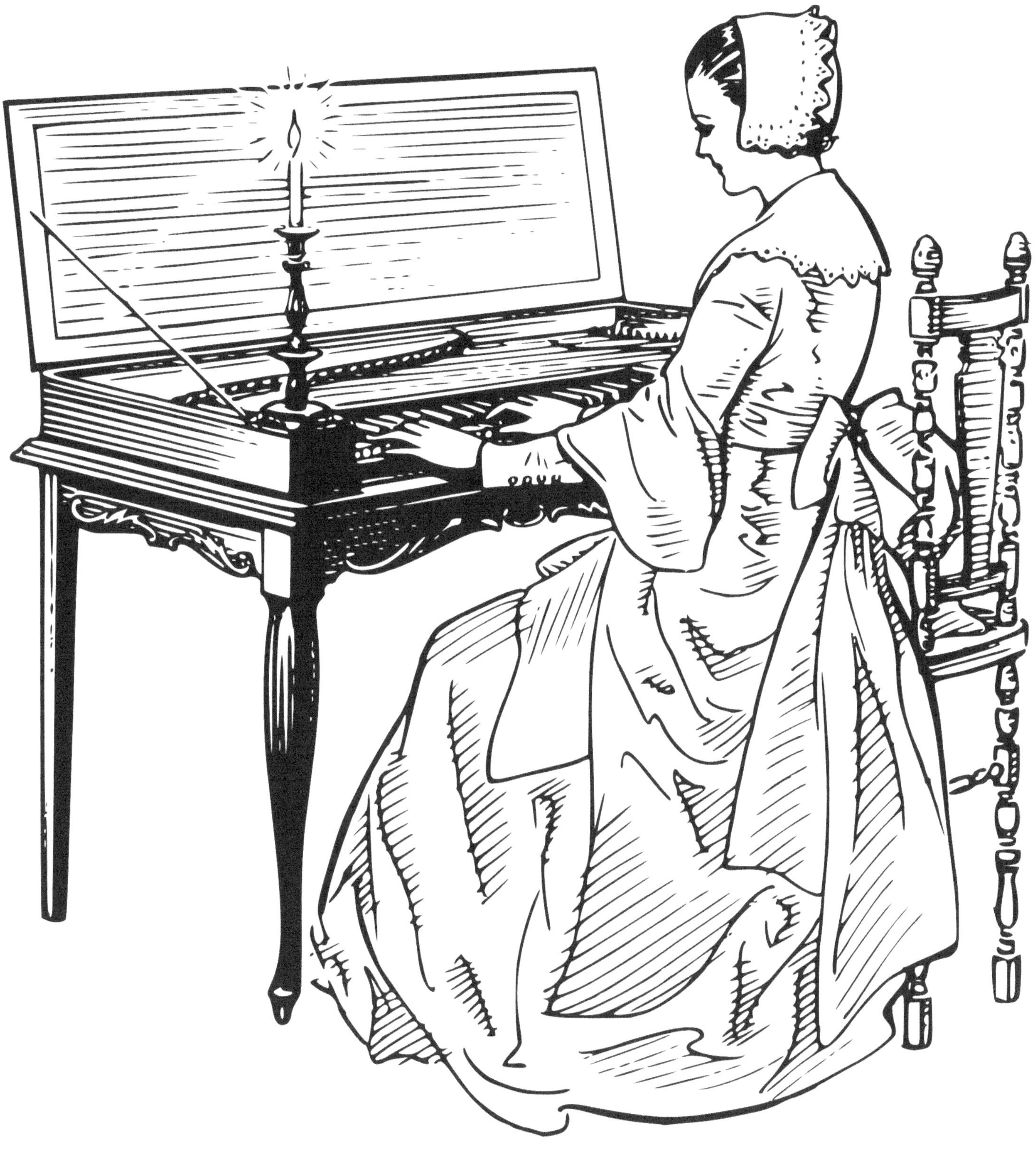

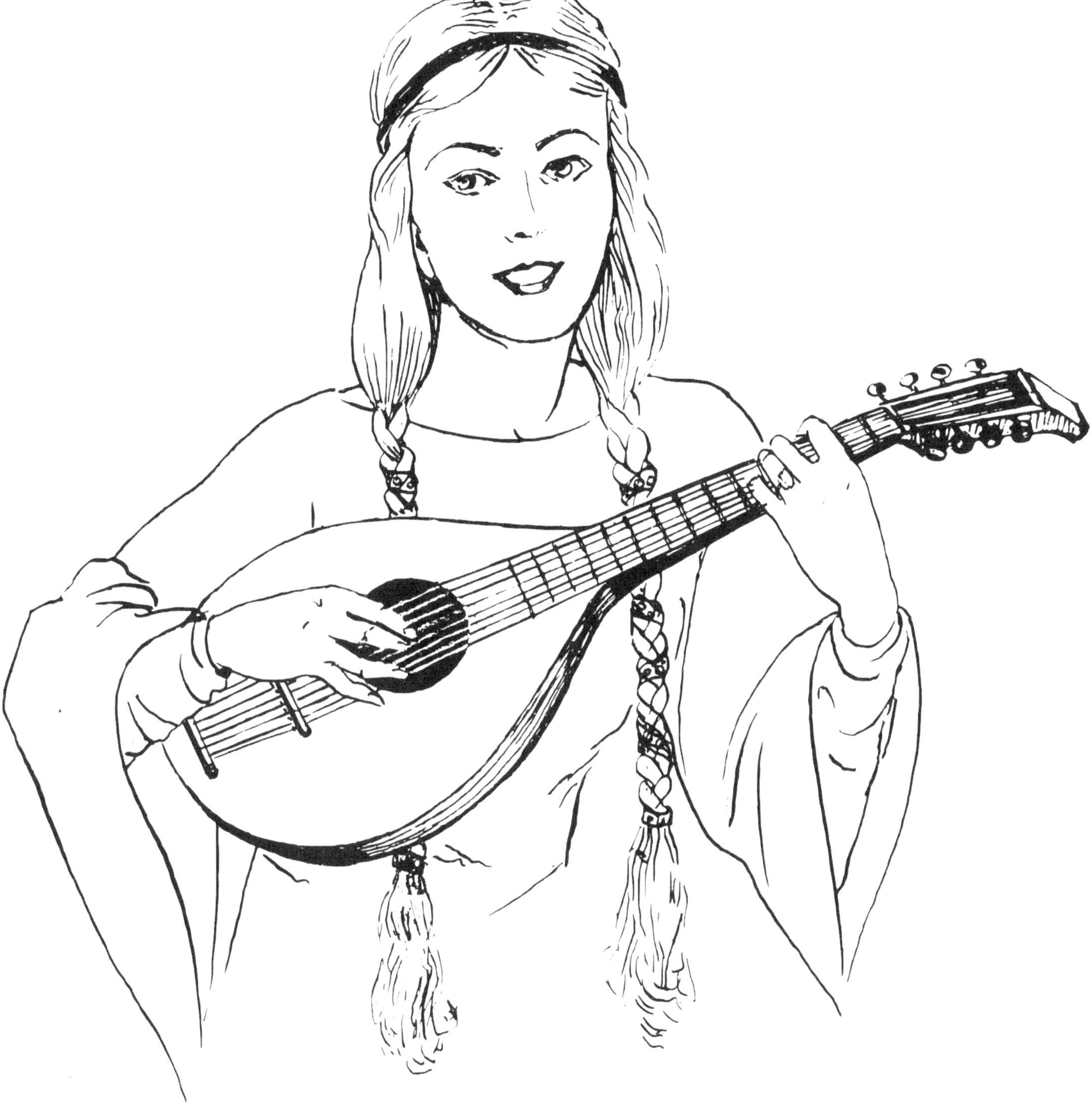

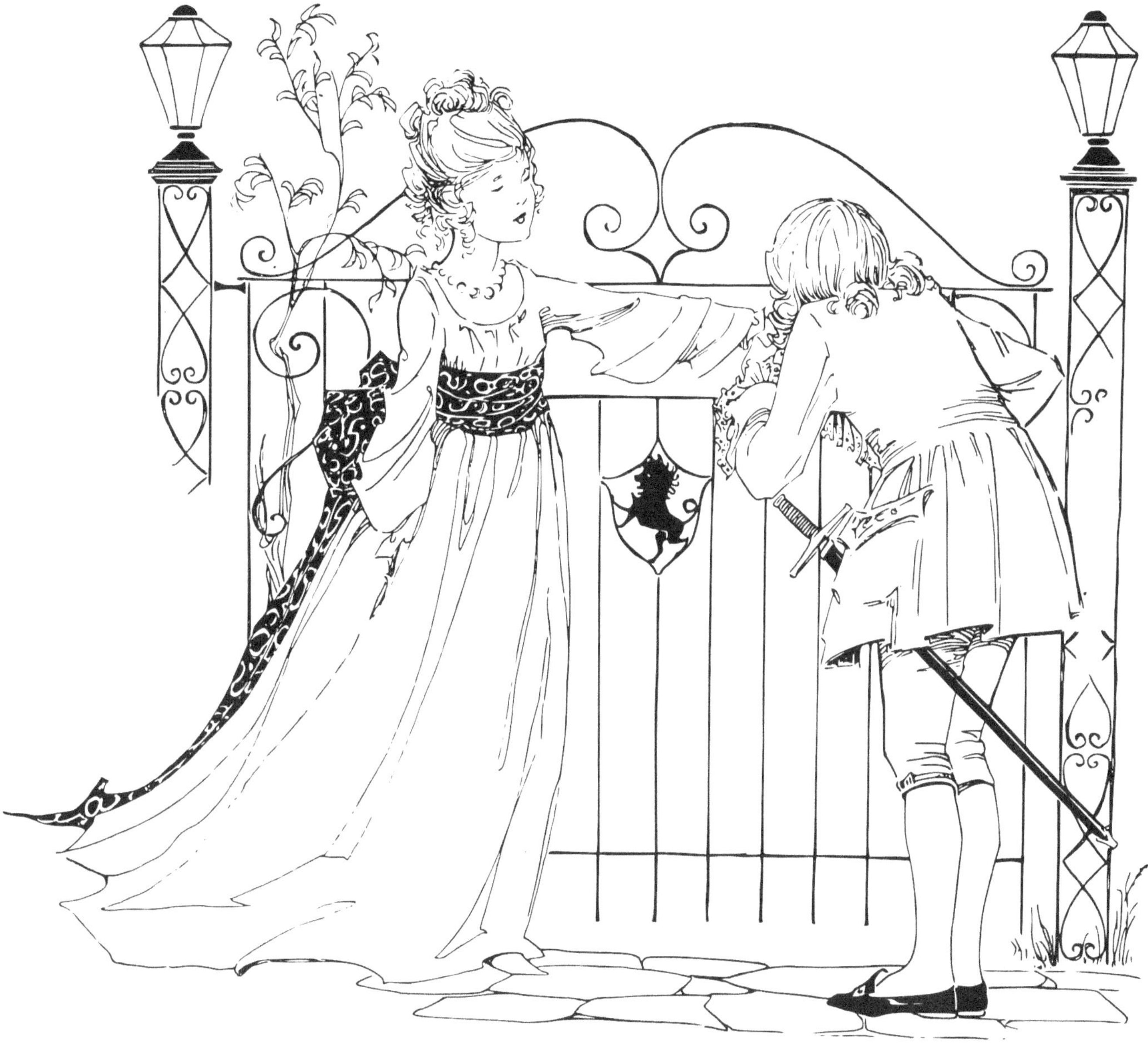

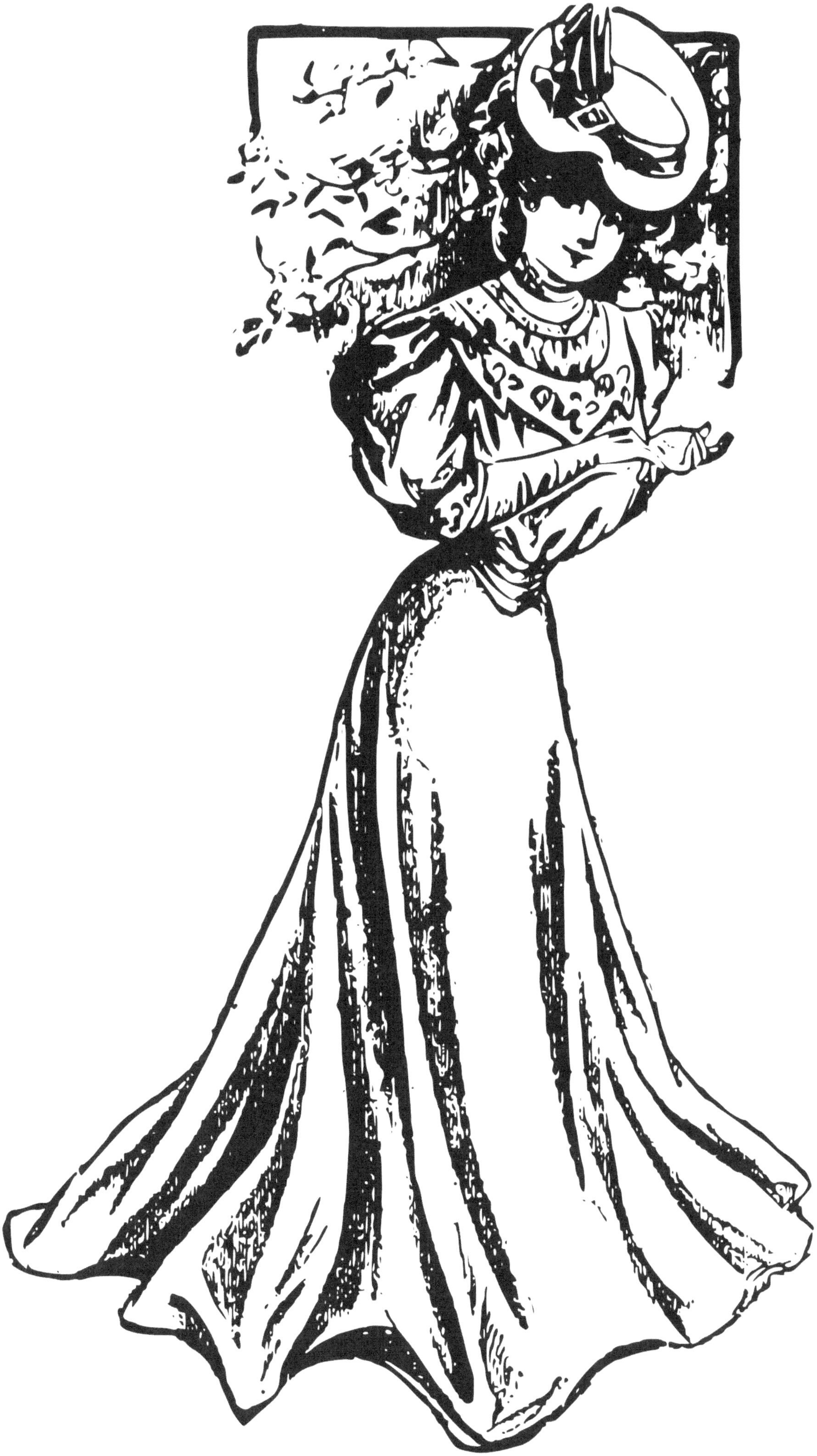

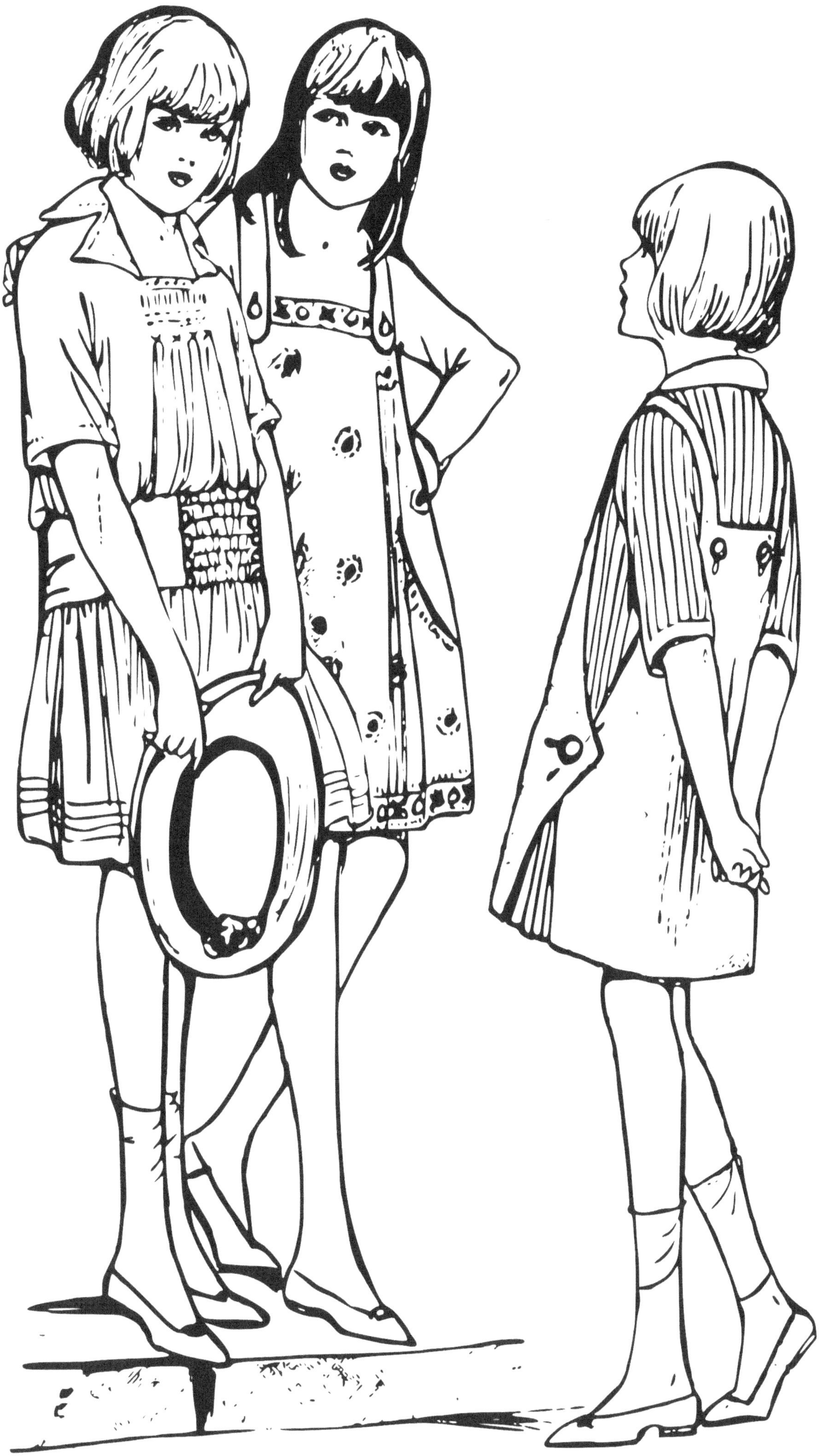

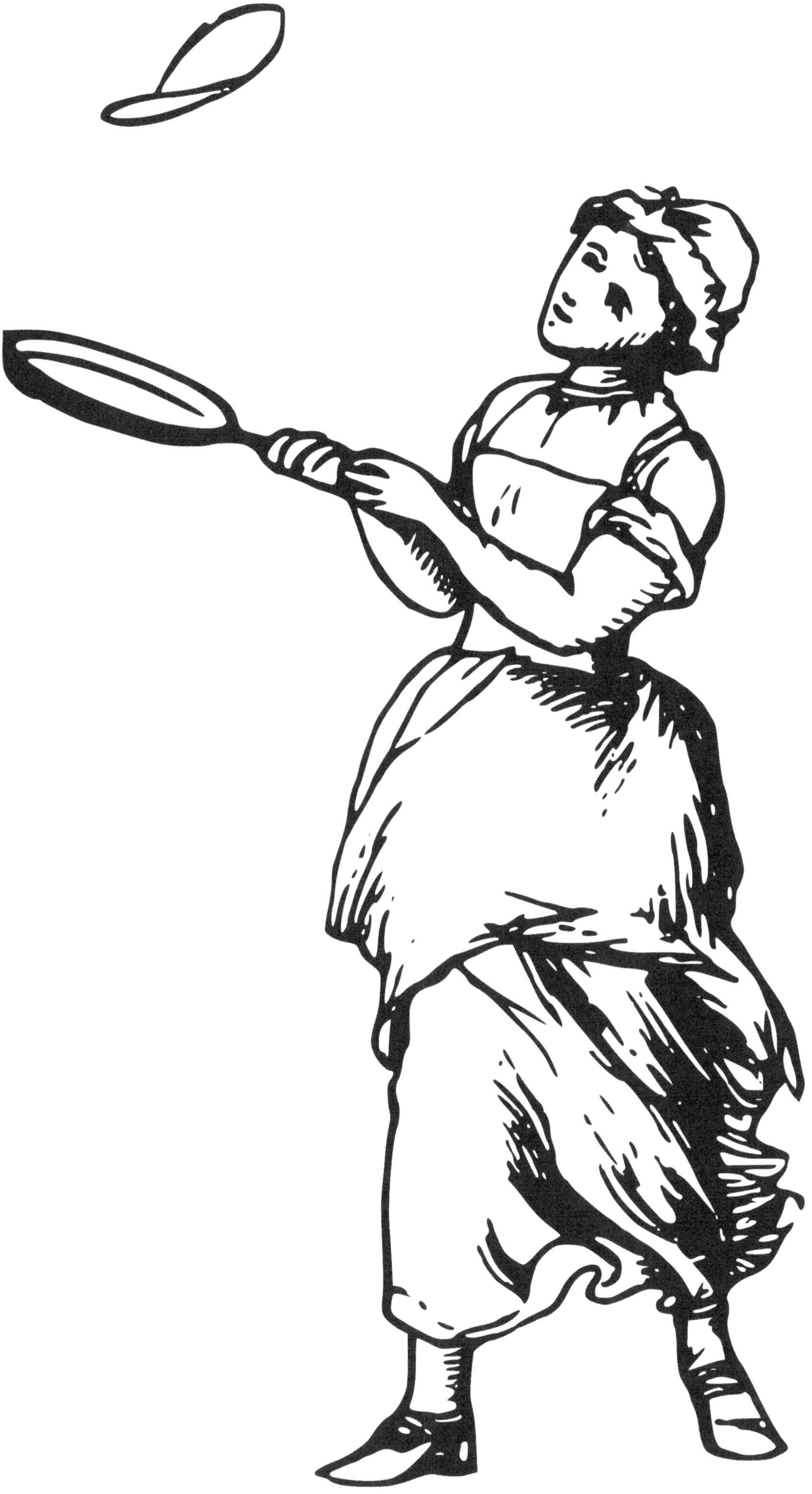

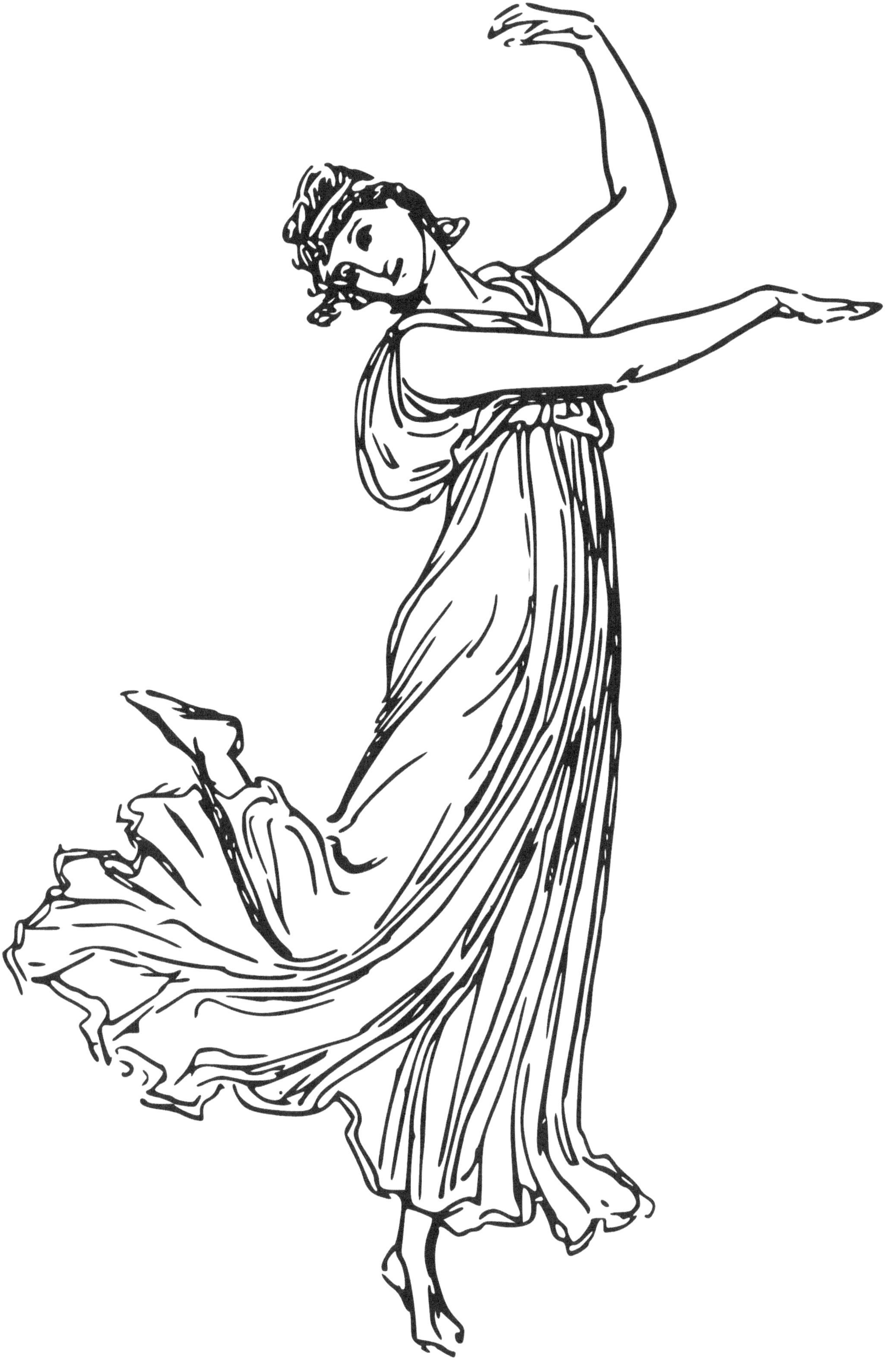

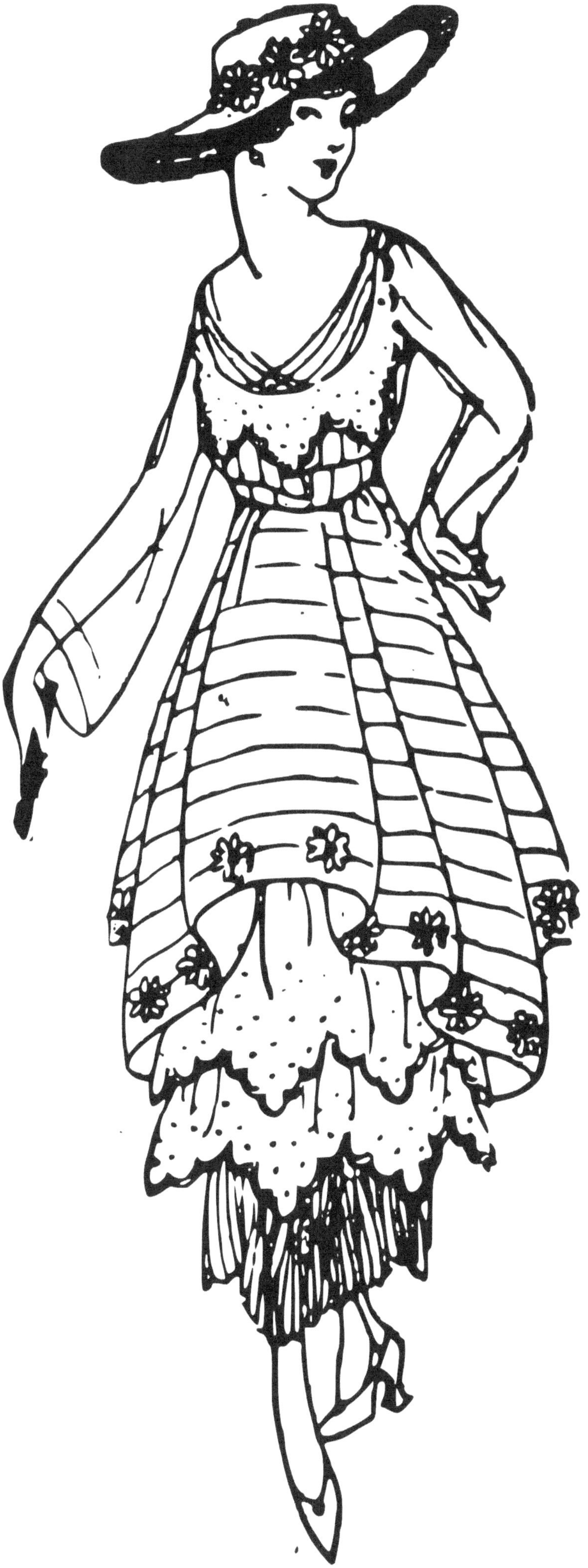

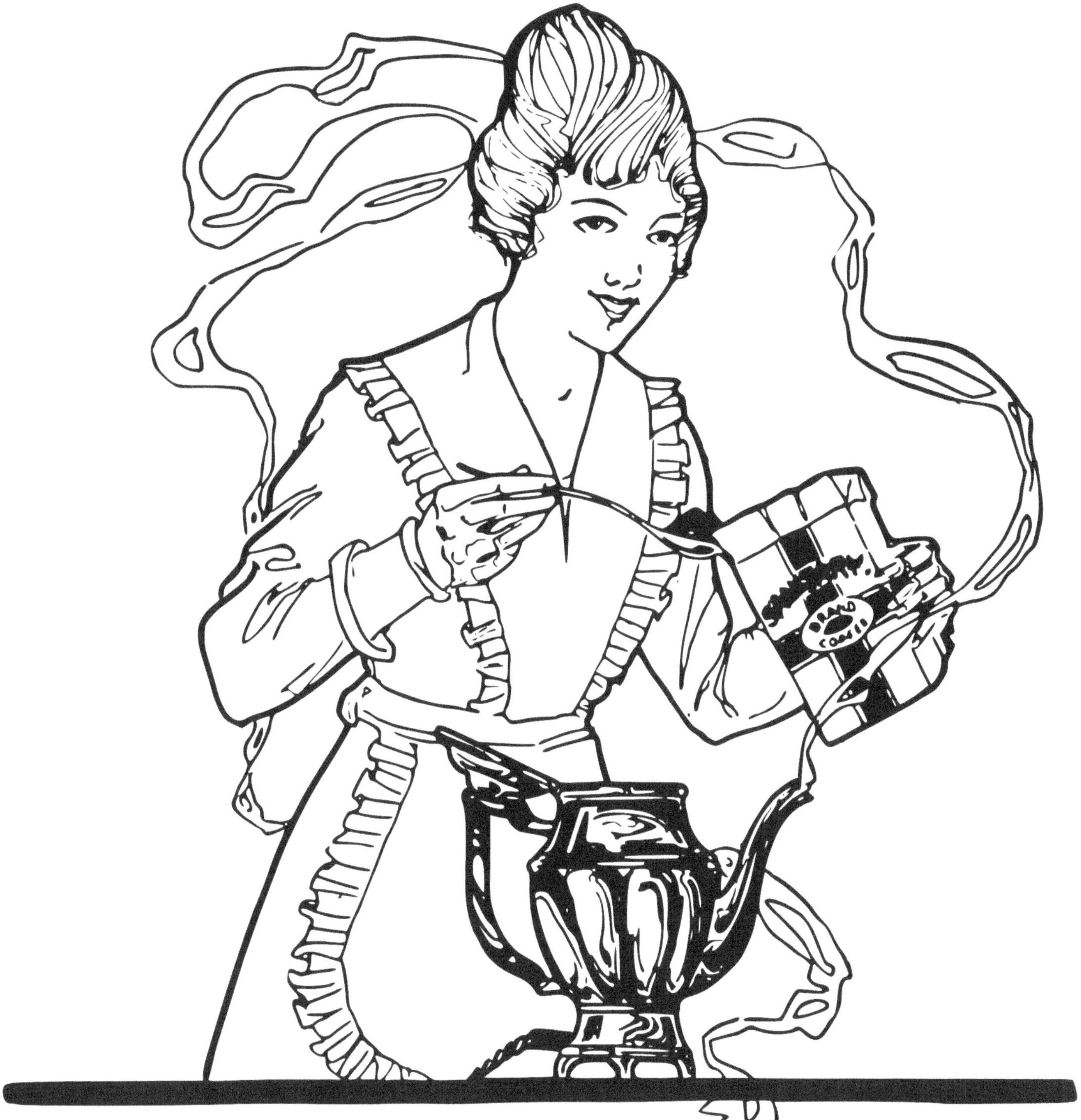
BRAND
COFFEE

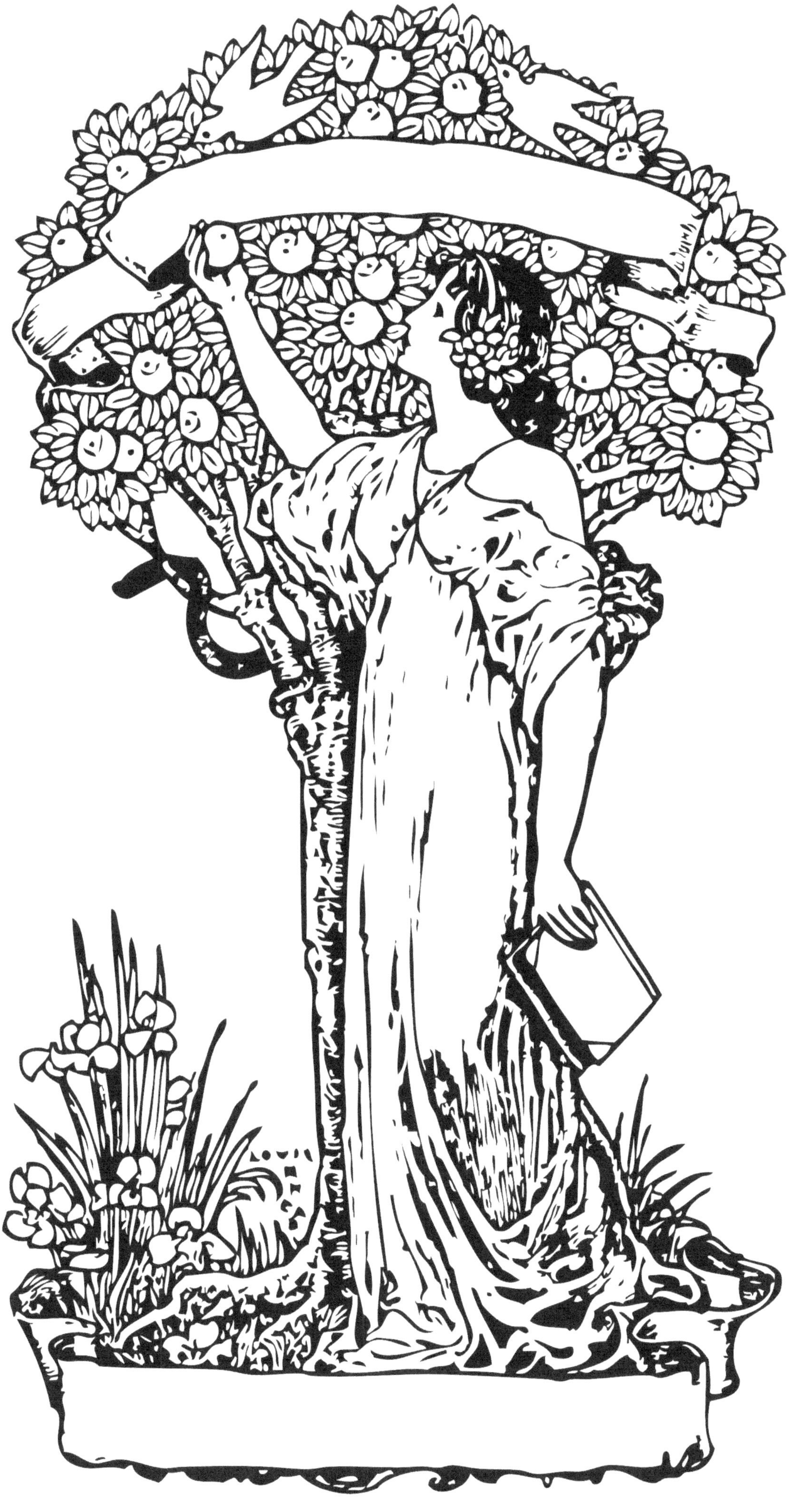

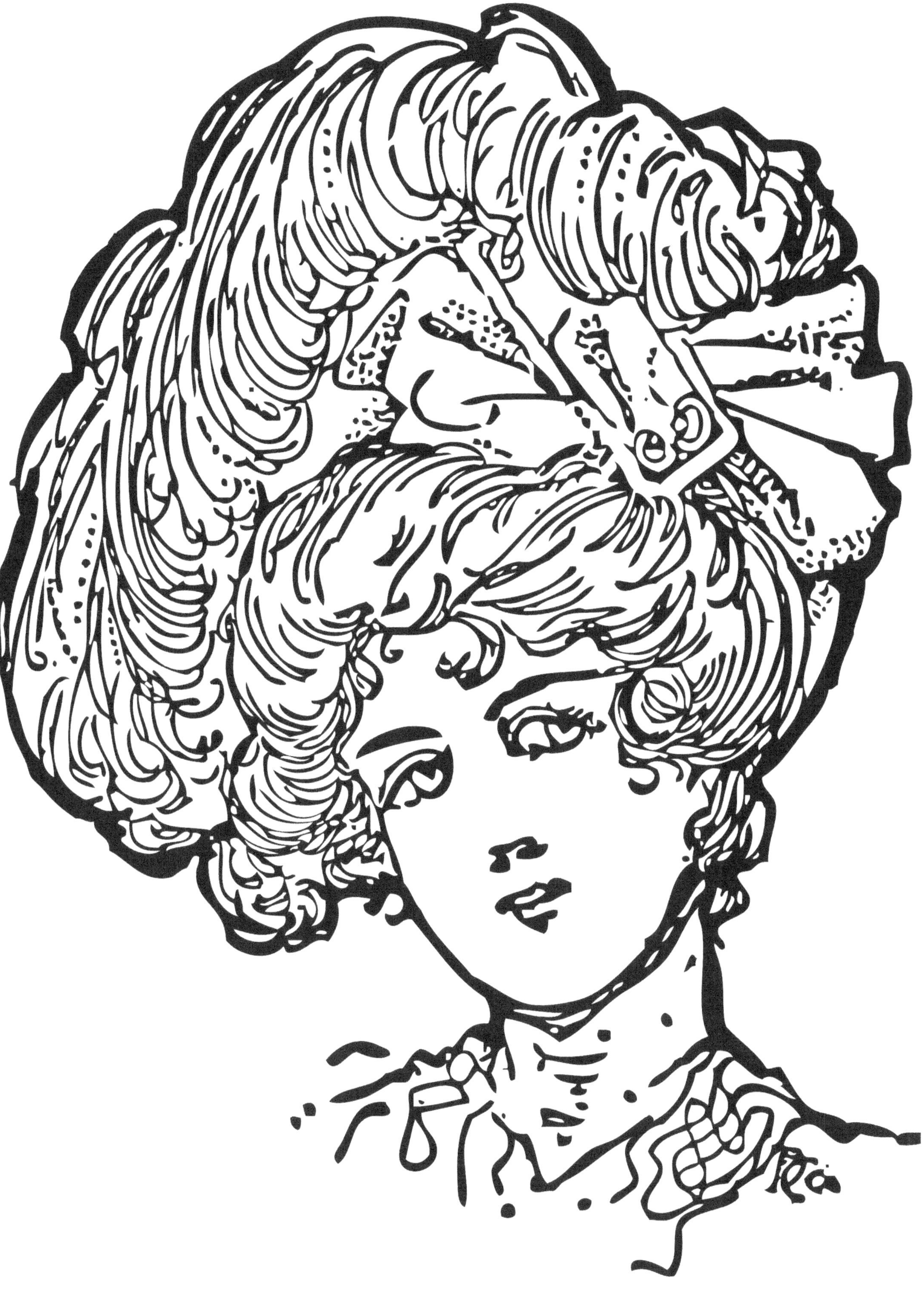

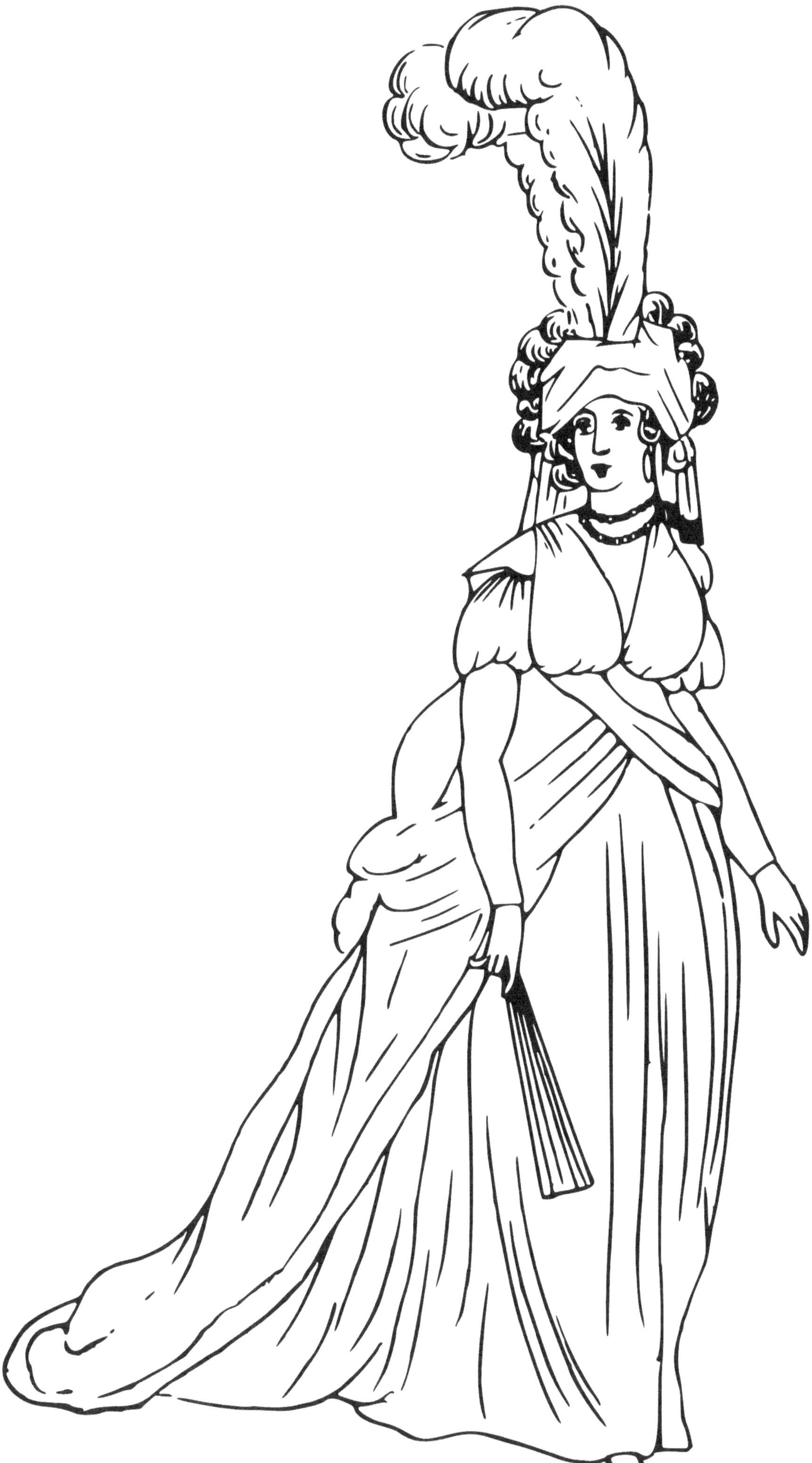

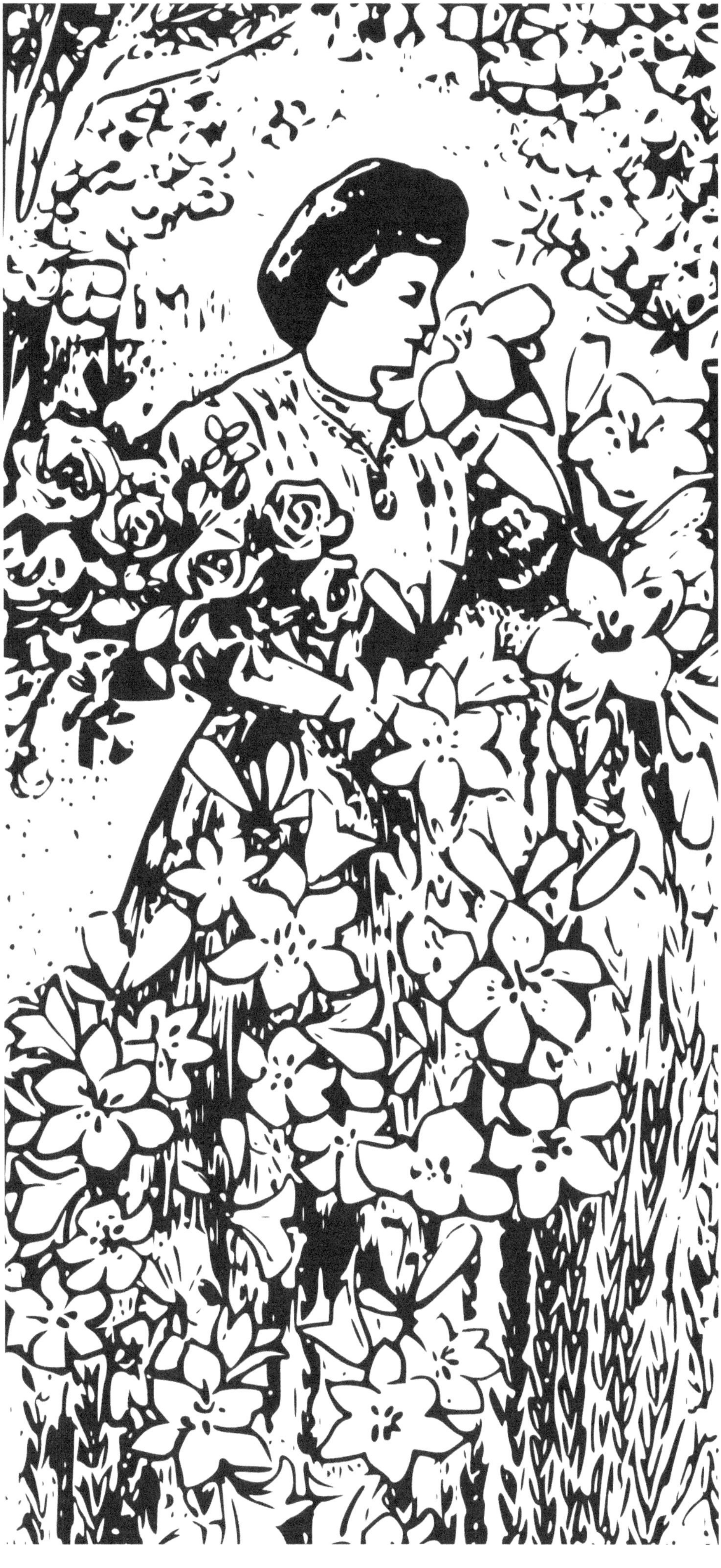

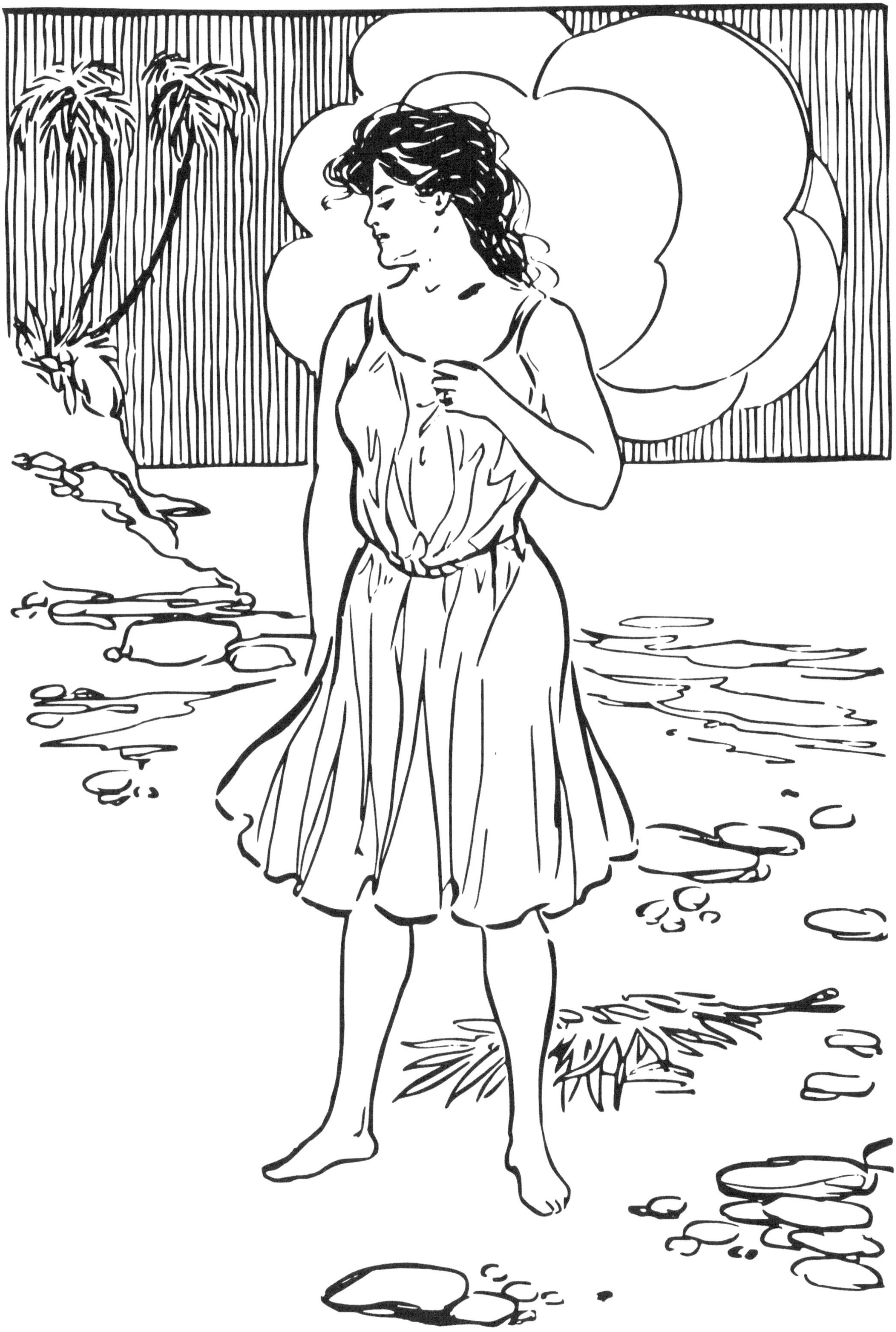

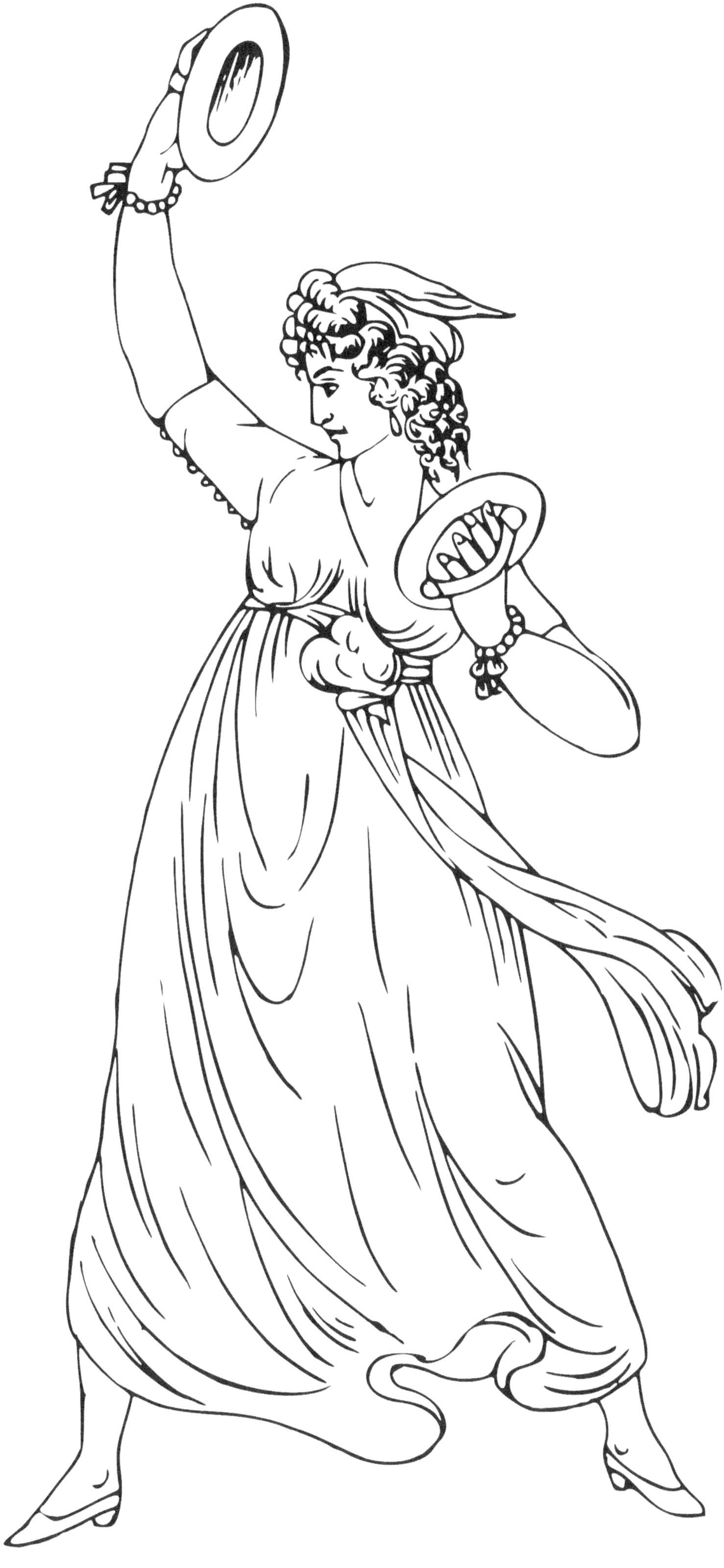

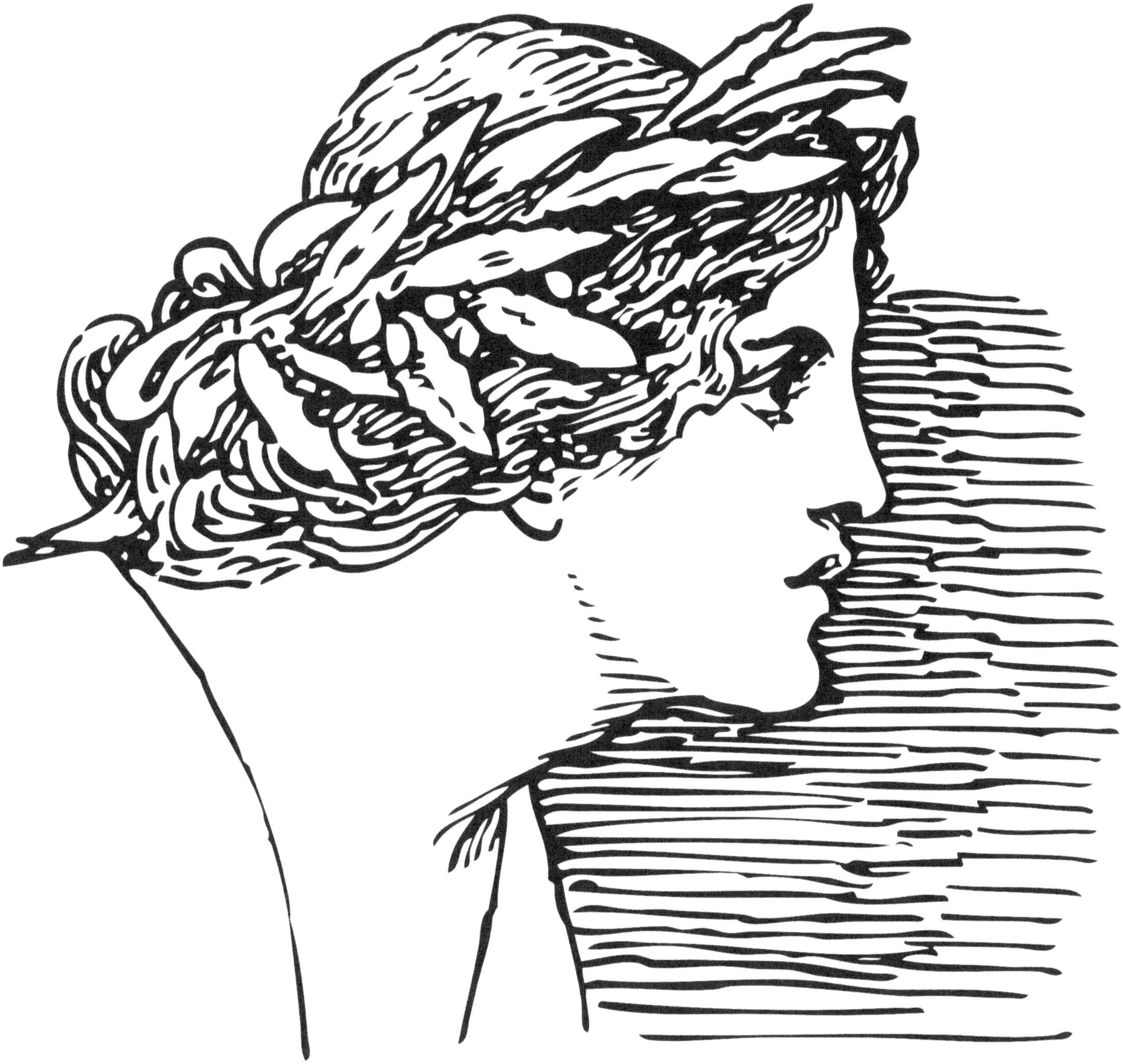

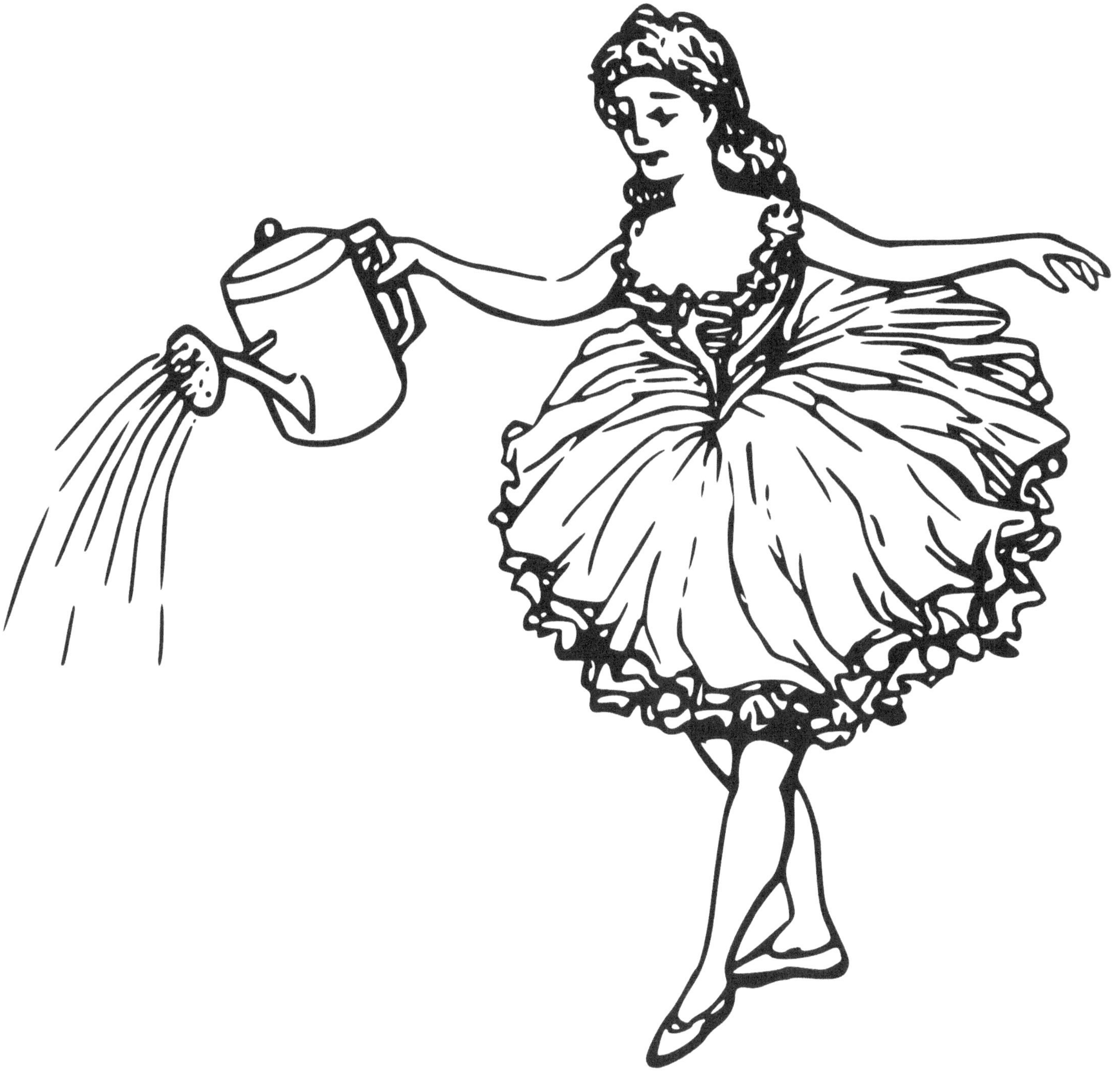

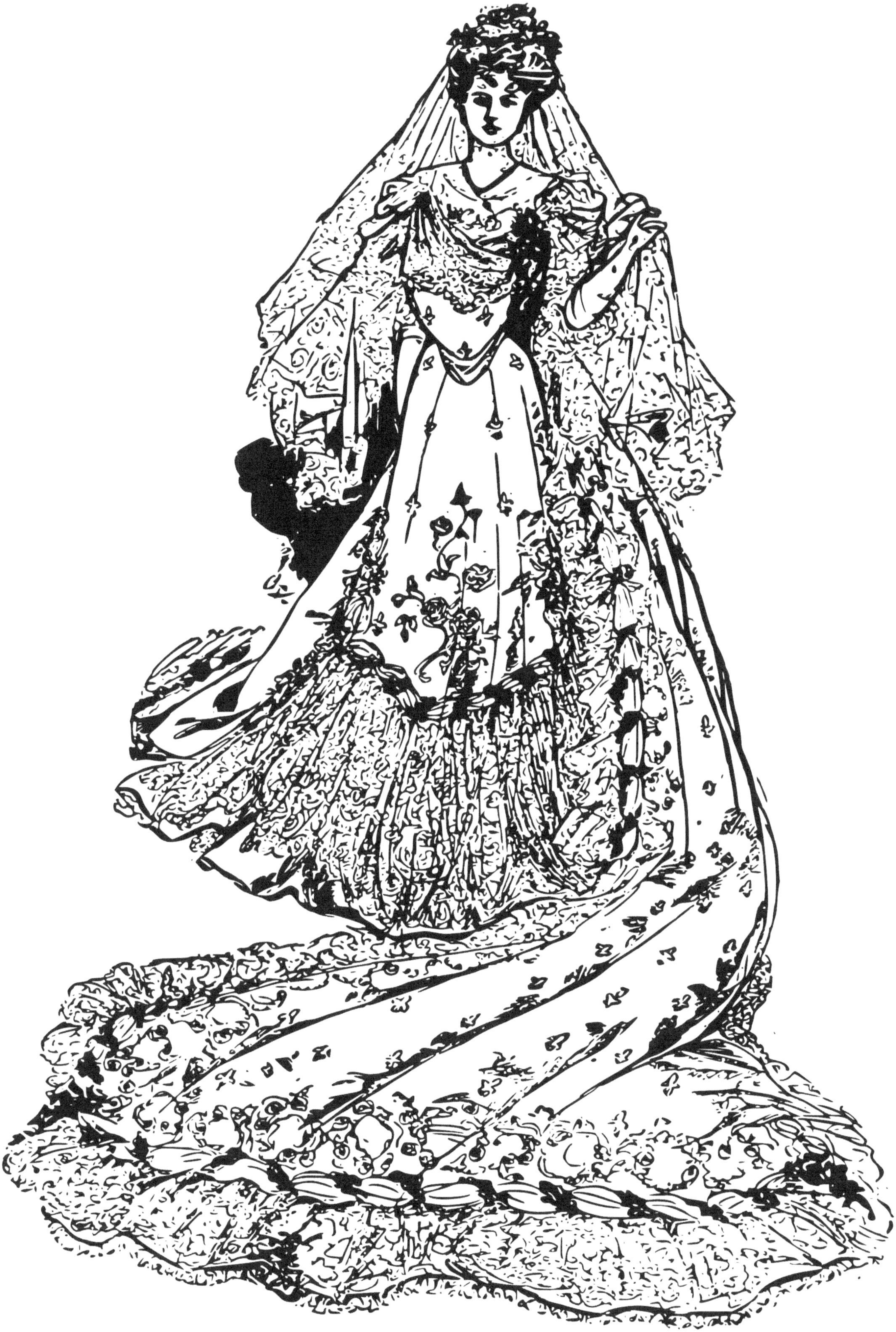

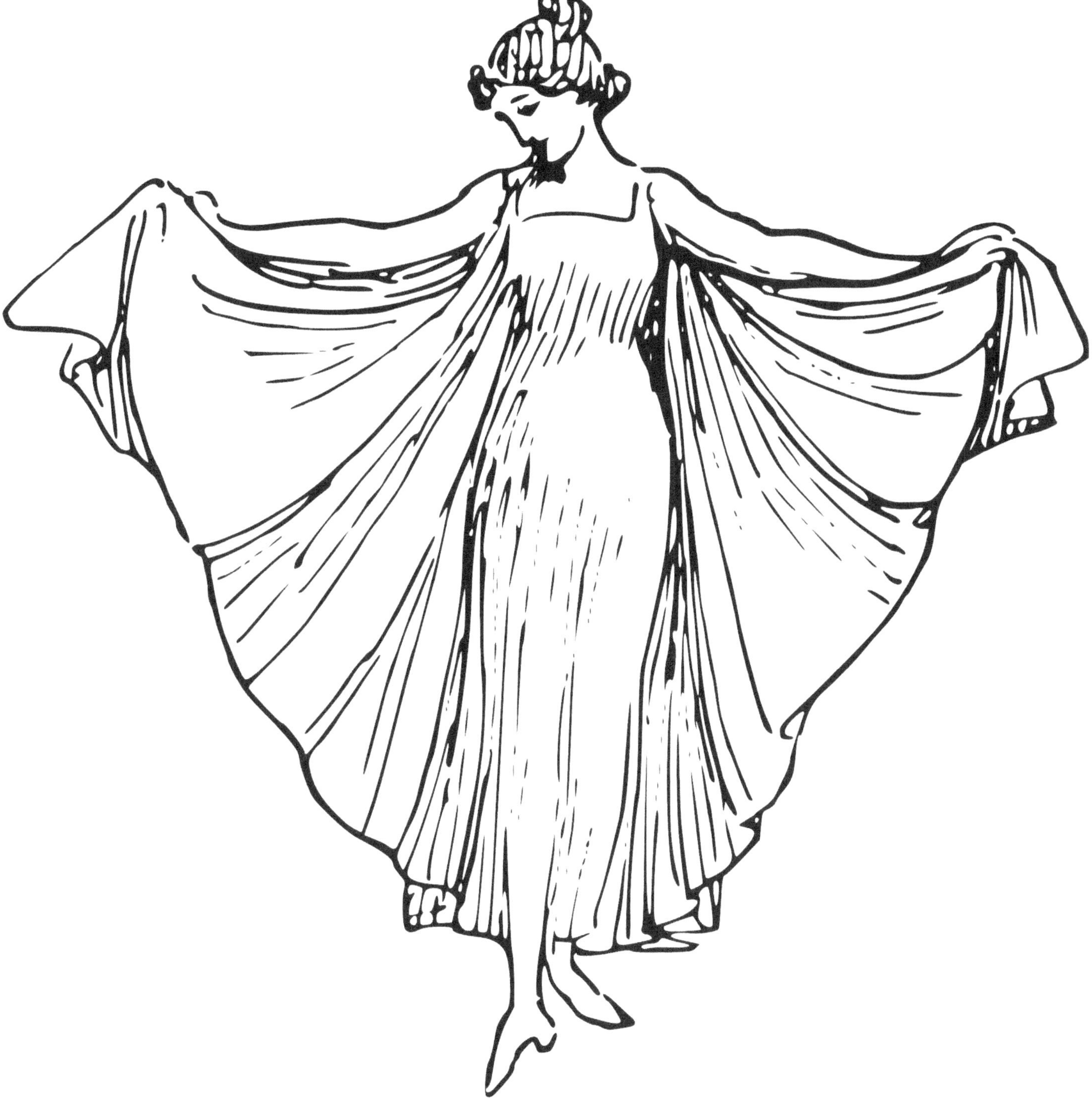

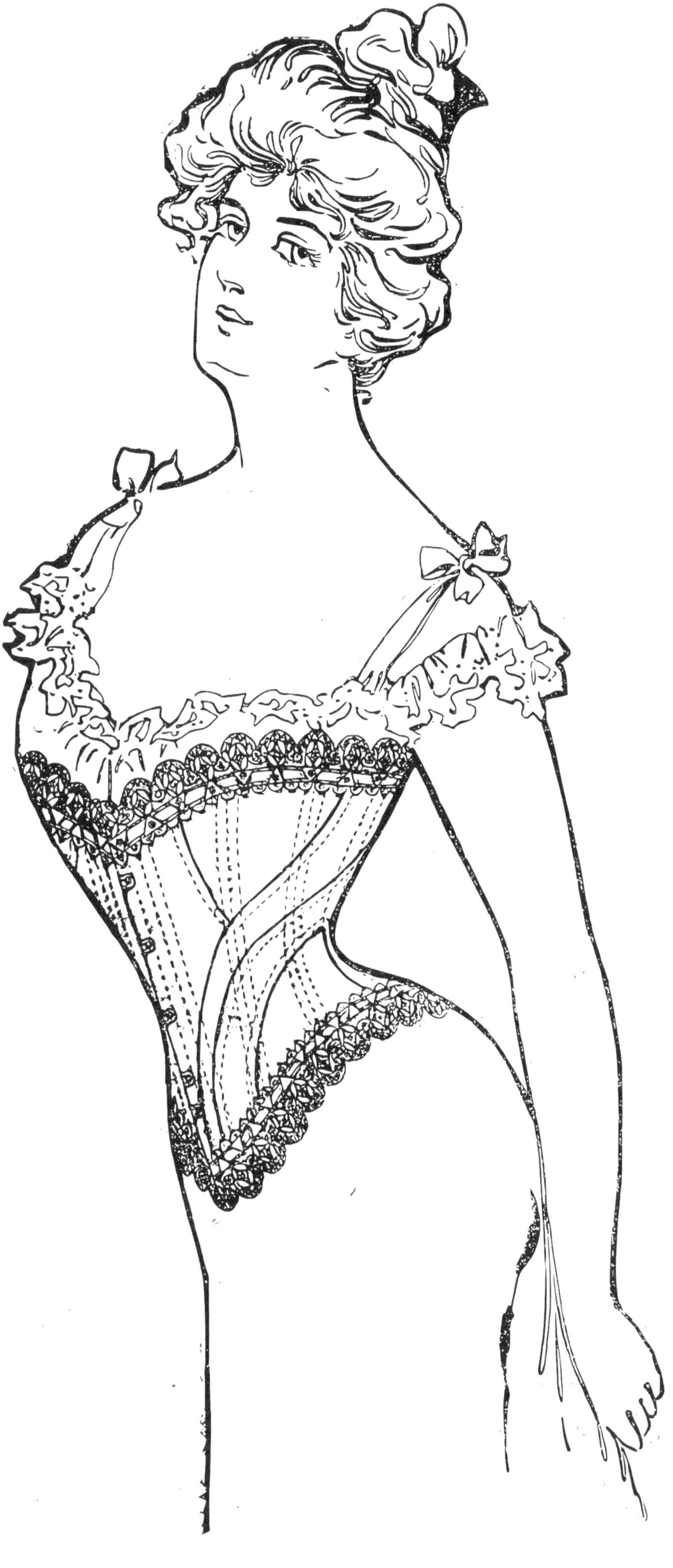

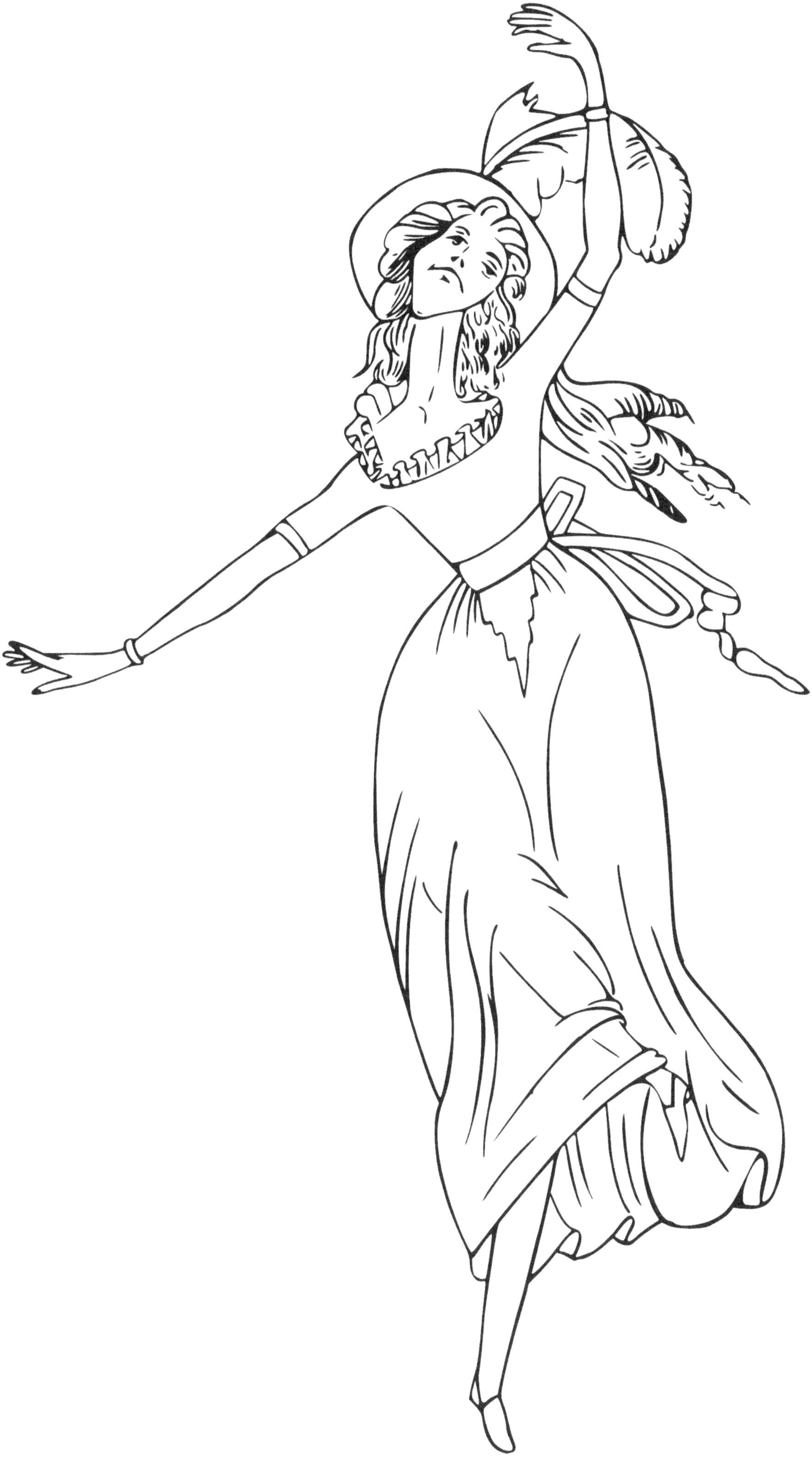

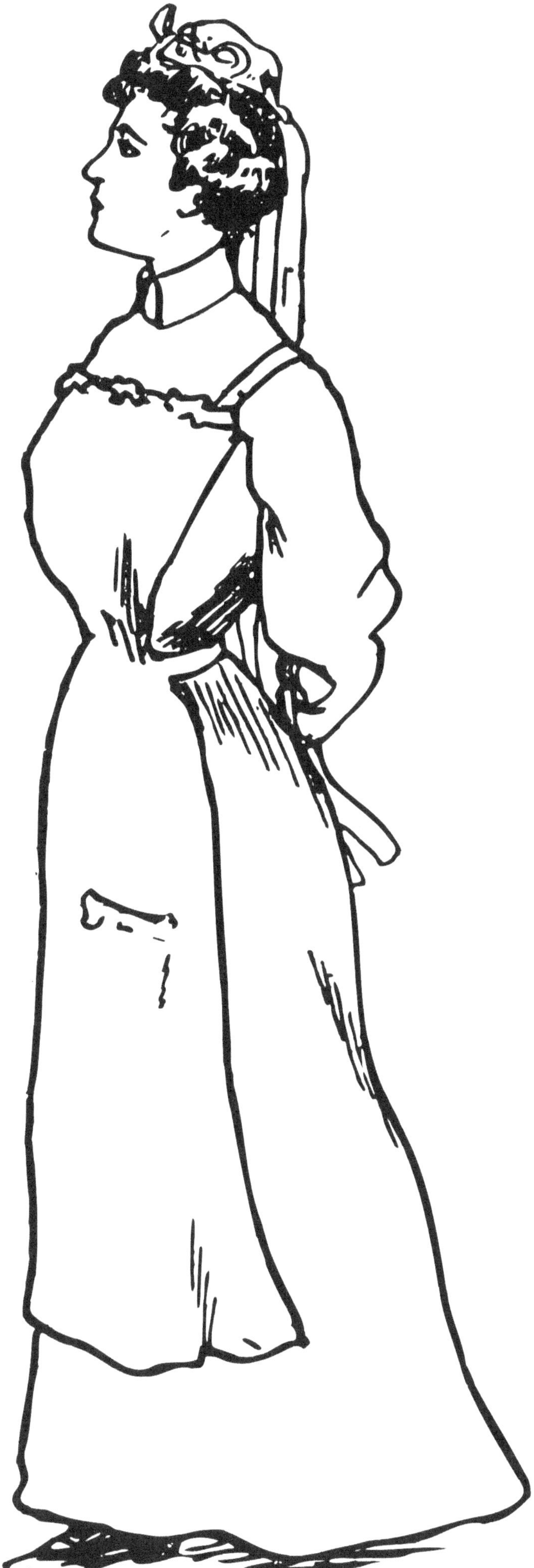

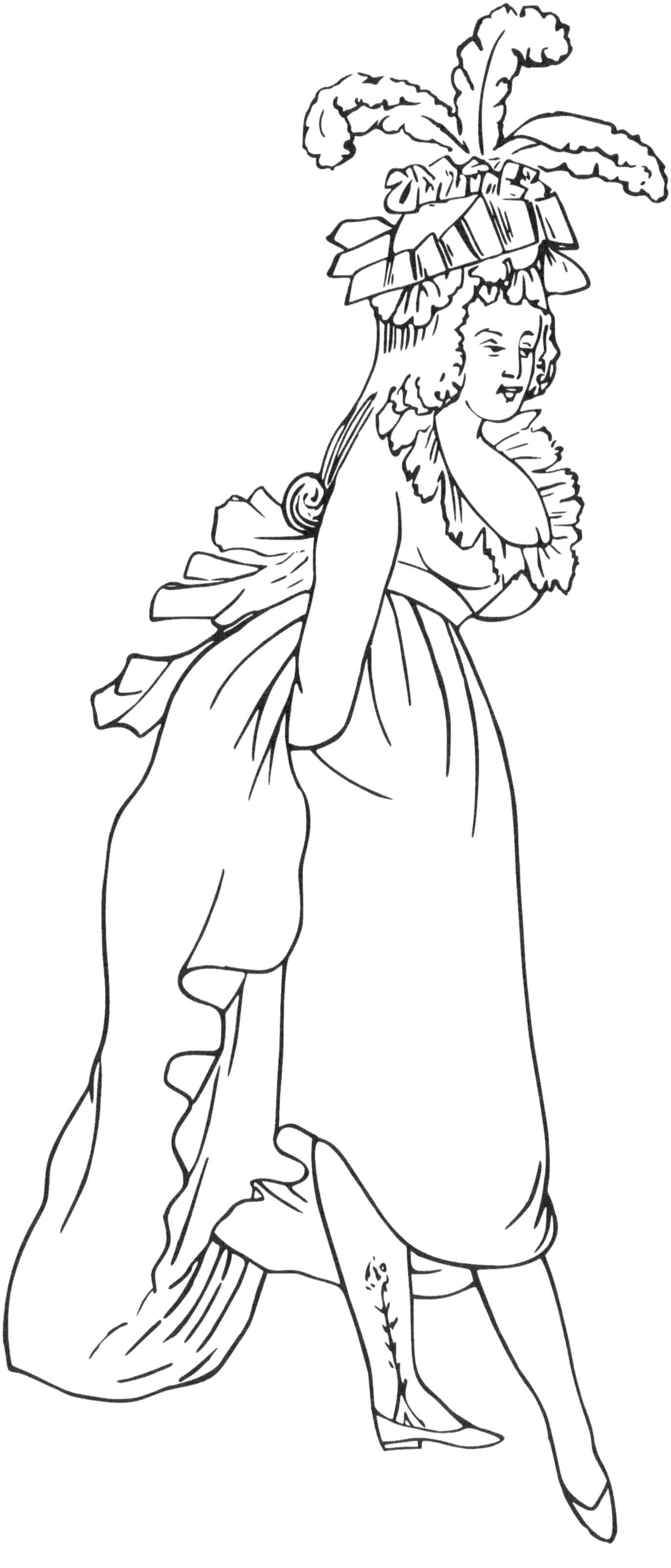

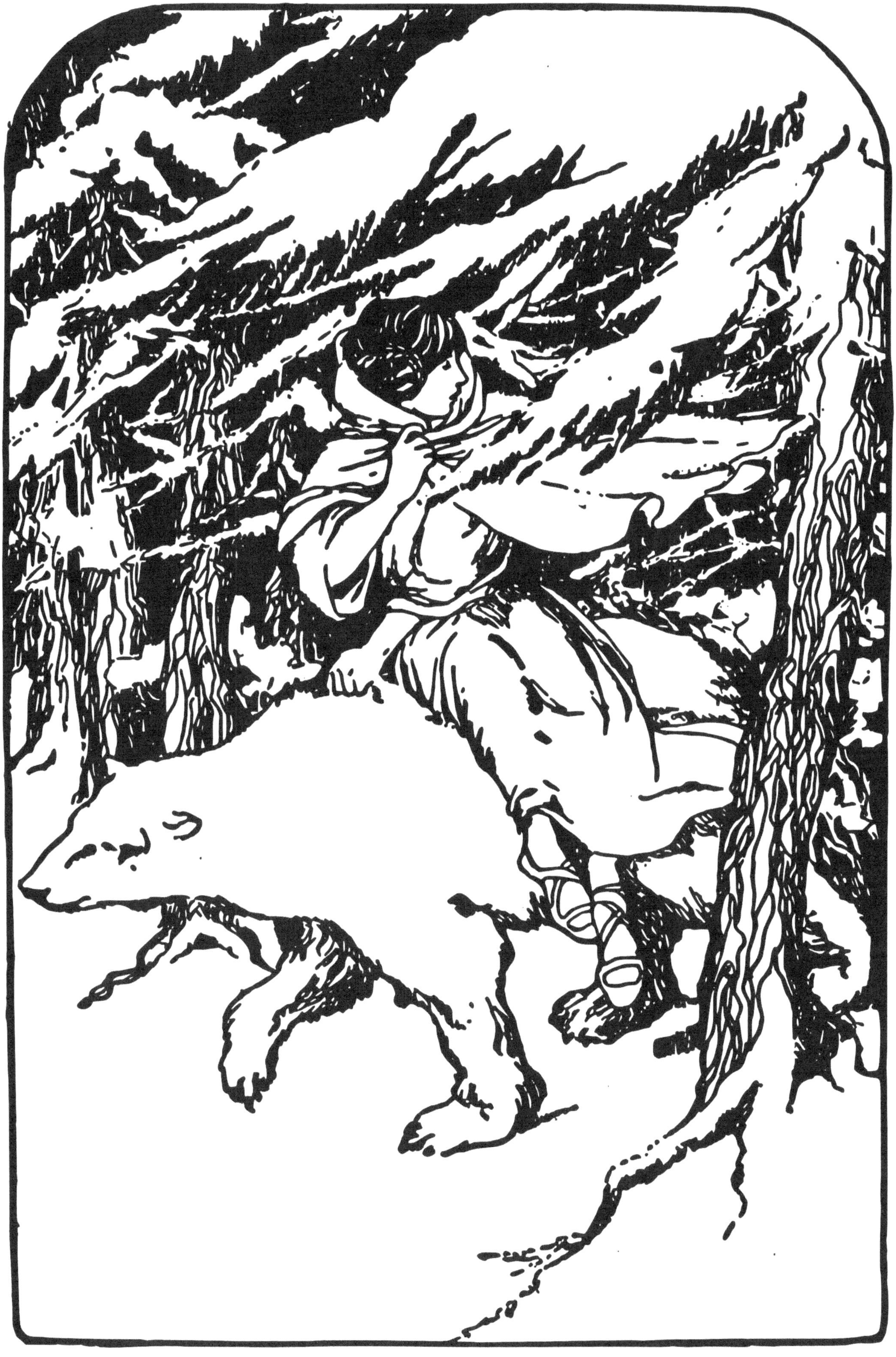

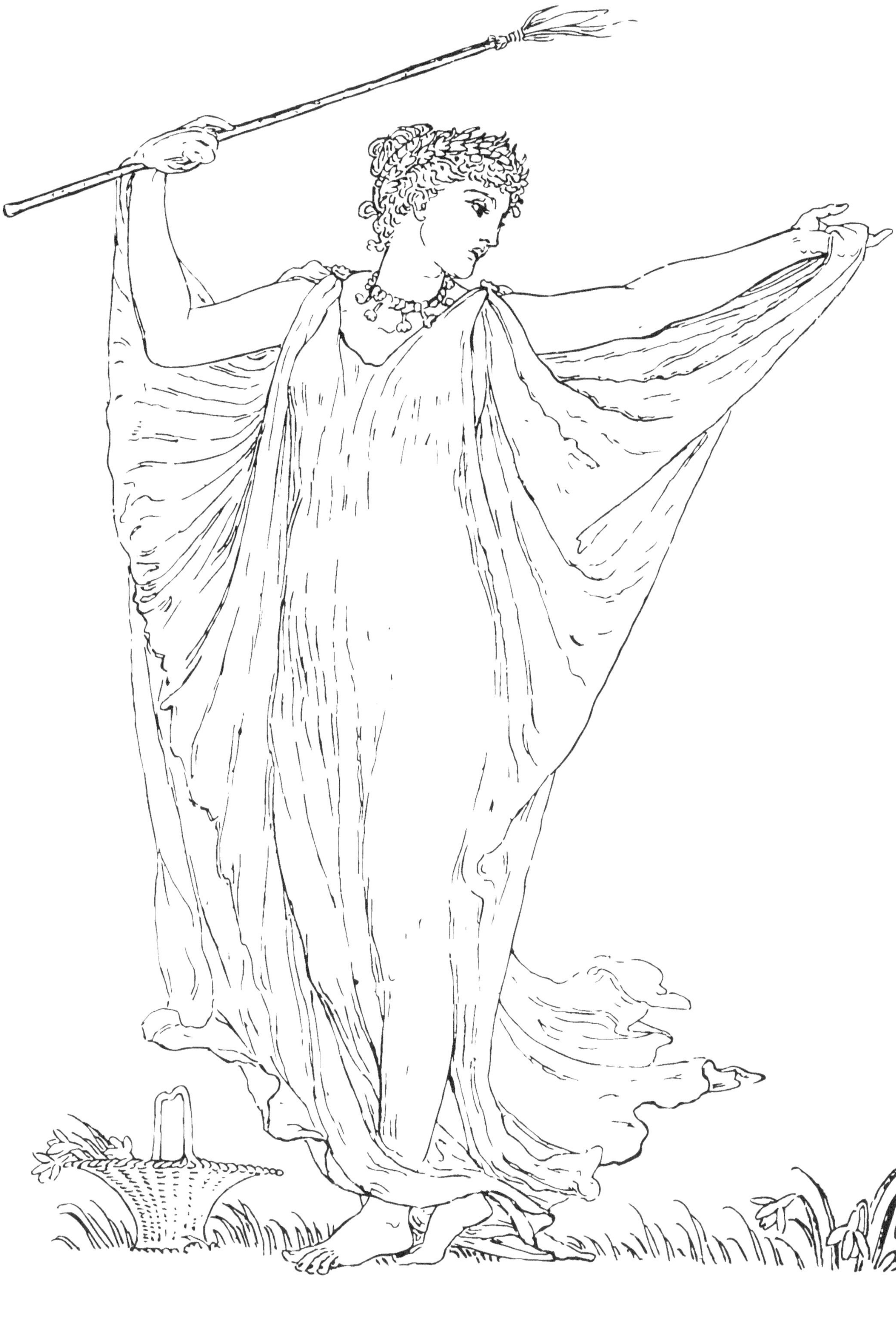

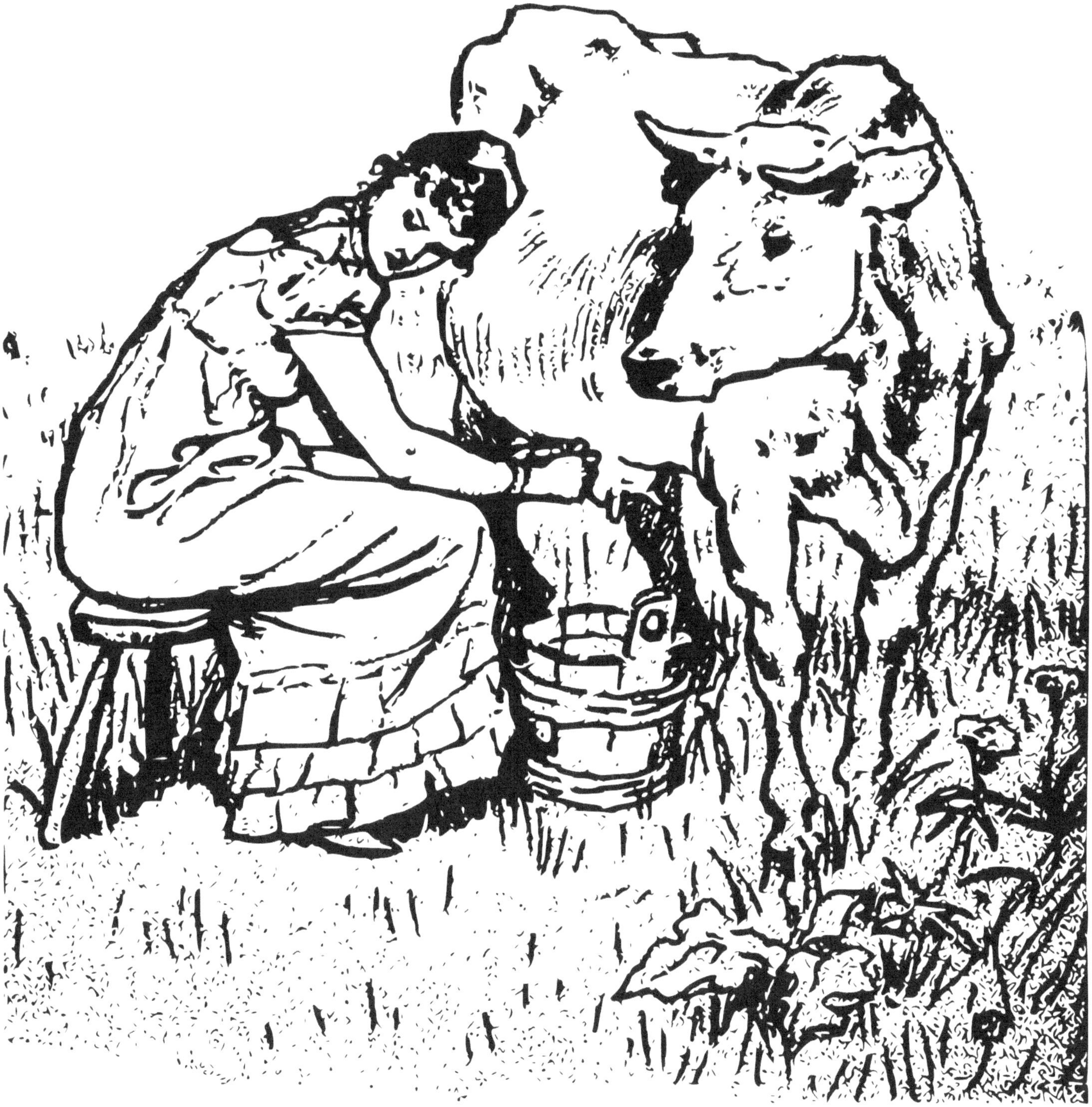

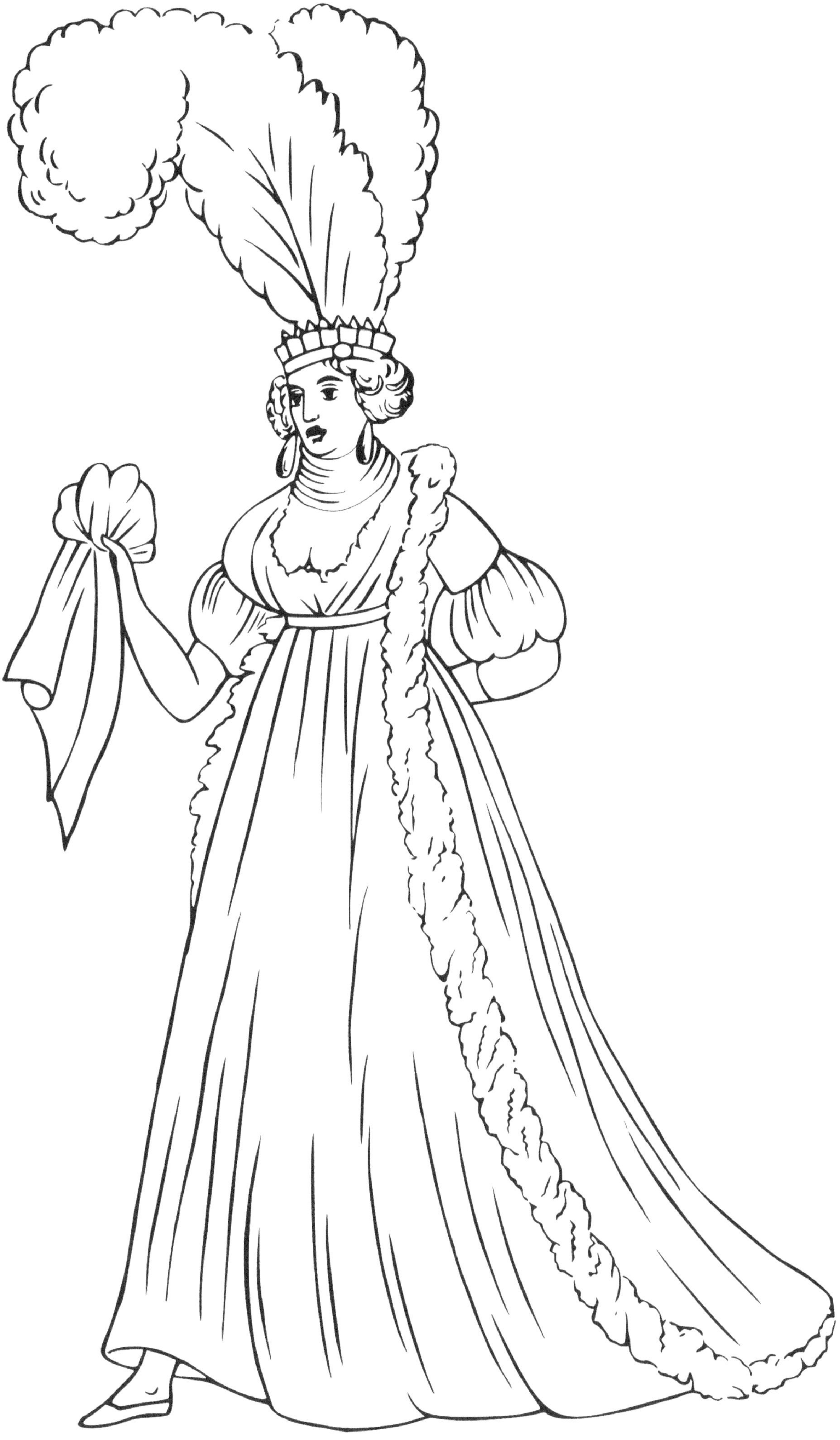

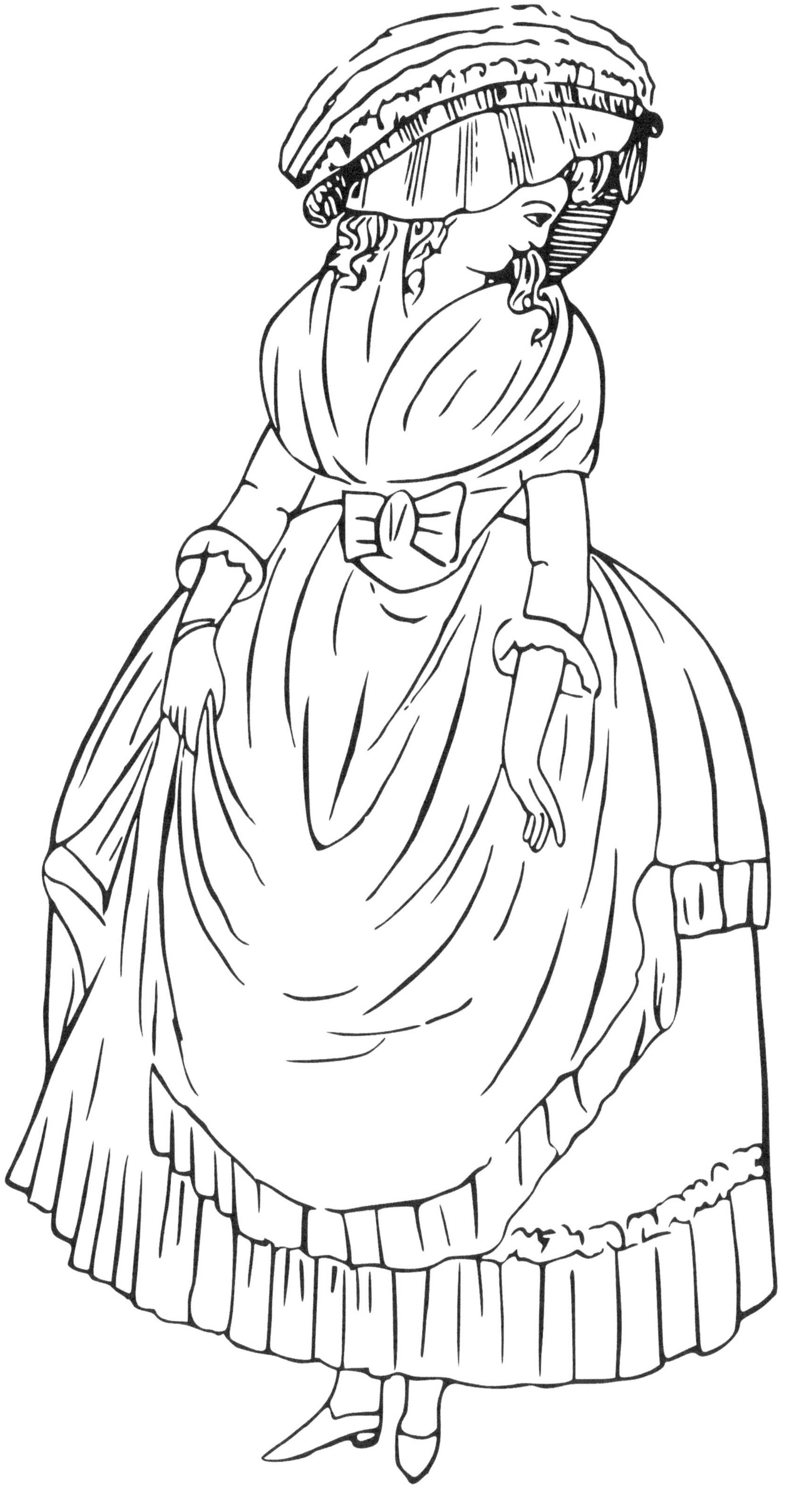

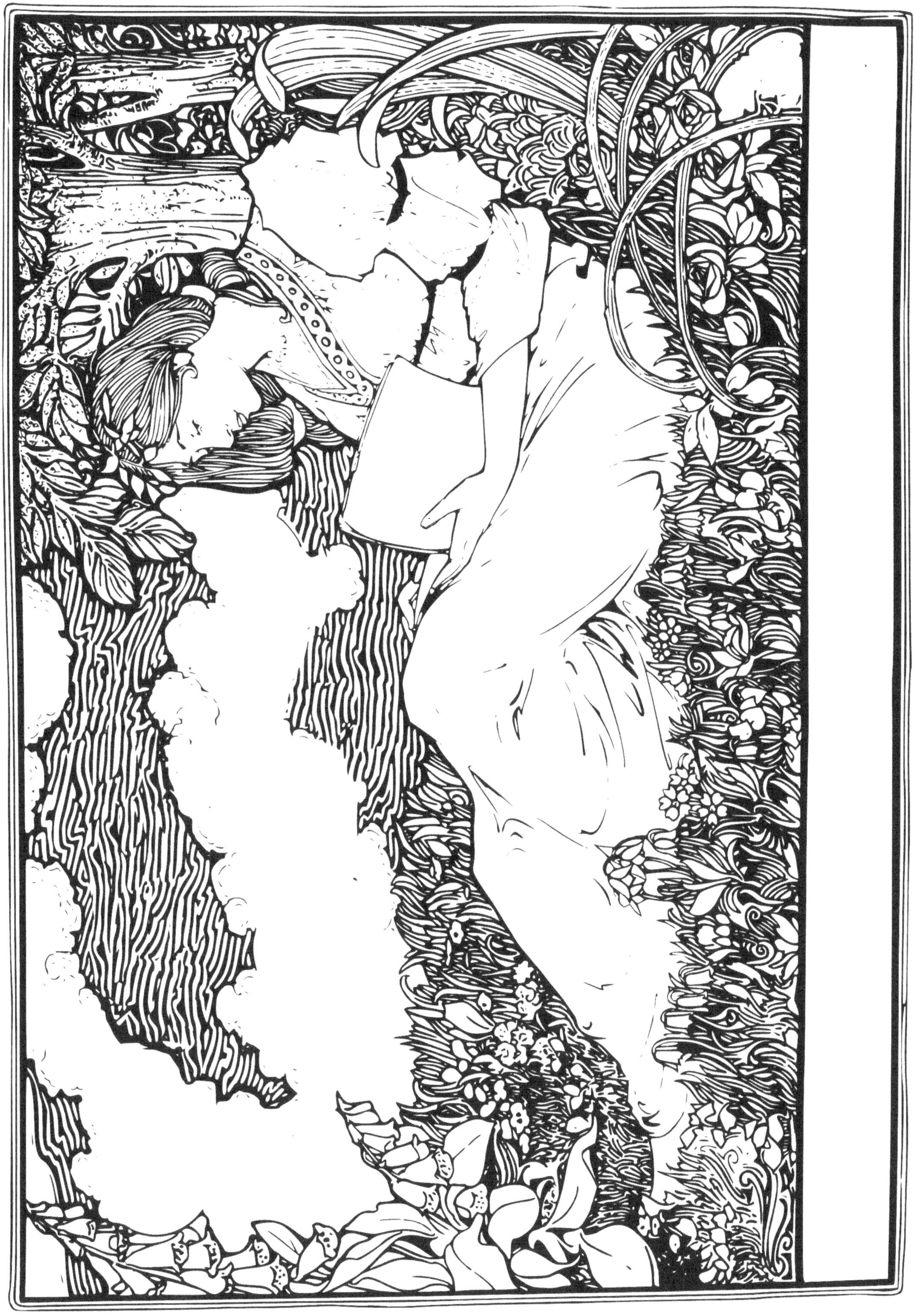

www.ingramcontent.com/pod-product-compliance
Lightning Source LLC
Chambersburg PA
CBHW080720190526
45169CB00006B/2453
* 9 7 8 1 5 3 2 7 5 4 0 6 7 *